THE WRITINGS

OF

JOHN BURROUGHS

I

WAKE-ROBIN

BOSTON AND NEW YORK

HOUGHTON MIFFLIN COMPANY

The Riverside Press Cambridge

Mr. Burroughs

PREFACE TO FIRST EDITION

THIS is mainly a book about the Birds, or more properly an invitation to the study of Ornithology, and the purpose of the author will be carried out in proportion as it awakens and stimulates the interest of the reader in this branch of Natural History.

Though written less in the spirit of exact science than with the freedom of love and old acquaintance, yet I have in no instance taken liberties with facts, or allowed my imagination to influence me to the extent of giving a false impression or a wrong coloring. I have reaped my harvest more in the woods than in the study; what I offer, in fact, is a careful and conscientious record of actual observations and experiences, and is true as it stands written, every word of it. But what has interested me most in Ornithology is the pursuit, the chase, the discovery; that part of it which is akin to hunting, fishing, and wild sports, and which I could carry with me in my eye and ear wherever I went.

I cannot answer with much confidence the poet's inquiry, —

" Hast thou named all the birds without a gun ? "

but I have done what I could to bring home the

"river and sky" with the sparrow I heard "singing at dawn on the alder bough." In other words, I have tried to present a live bird, — a bird in the woods or the fields, — with the atmosphere and associations of the place, and not merely a stuffed and labeled specimen.

A more specific title for the volume would have suited me better; but not being able to satisfy myself in this direction, I cast about for a word thoroughly in the atmosphere and spirit of the book, which I hope I have found in "Wake-Robin," the common name of the white Trillium, which blooms in all our woods, and which marks the arrival of all the birds.

CONTENTS

LIST OF ILLUSTRATIONS

INTRODUCTION TO RIVERSIDE EDITION

In coming before the public with a newly made edition of my writings, what can I say to my reader at this stage of our acquaintance that will lead to a better understanding between us? Probably nothing. We understand each other very well already. I have offered myself as his guide to certain matters out of doors, and to a few matters indoors, and he has accepted me upon my own terms, and has, on the whole, been better pleased with me than I had any reason to expect. For this I am duly grateful; why say more? Yet, now that I am upon my feet, so to speak, and palaver is the order, I will keep on a few minutes longer.

It is now nearly a quarter of a century since my first book, "Wake-Robin," was published. I have lived nearly as many years in the world as I had lived when I wrote its principal chapters. Other volumes have followed, and still others. When asked how many there are, I often have to stop and count them up. I suppose the mother of a large family does not have to count up her children to say how many there are. She sees their faces all before her. It is said of certain savage tribes

who cannot count above five, and yet who own
flocks and herds, that every native knows when he
has got all his own cattle, not by counting, but by
remembering each one individually.

The savage is with his herds daily; the mother
has the love of her children constantly in her heart;
but when one's book goes forth from him, in a sense
it never returns. It is like the fruit detached from
the bough. And yet to sit down and talk of one's
books as a father might talk of his sons, who had
left his roof and gone forth to make their own way
in the world, is not an easy matter. The author's
relation to his book is a little more direct and personal, after all, more a matter of will and choice,
than a father's relation to his child. The book
does not change, and, whatever its fortunes, it remains to the end what its author made it. The
son is an evolution out of a long line of ancestry,
and one's responsibility for this or that trait is often
very slight; but the book is an actual transcript of
his mind, and is wise or foolish according as he made
it so. Hence I trust my reader will pardon me if I
shrink from any discussion of the merits or demerits
of these intellectual children of mine, or indulge in
any very confidential remarks with regard to them.

I cannot bring myself to think of my books as
"works," because so little "work" has gone to the
making of them. It has all been play. I have
gone a-fishing, or camping, or canoeing, and new

INTRODUCTION

literary material has been the result. My corn has grown while I loitered or slept. The writing of the book was only a second and finer enjoyment of my holiday in the fields or woods. Not till the writing did it really seem to strike in and become part of me.

A friend of mine, now an old man, who spent his youth in the woods of northern Ohio, and who has written many books, says, " I never thought of writing a book till my self-exile, and then only to reproduce my old-time life to myself." The writing probably cured or alleviated a sort of homesickness. Such in a great measure has been my own case. My first book, " Wake-Robin," was written while I was a government clerk in Washington. It enabled me to live over again the days I had passed with the birds and in the scenes of my youth. I wrote the book sitting at a desk in front of an iron wall. I was the keeper of a vault in which many millions of bank-notes were stored. During my long periods of leisure I took refuge in my pen. How my mind reacted from the iron wall in front of me, and sought solace in memories of the birds and of summer fields and woods! Most of the chapters of "Winter Sunshine" were written at the same desk. The sunshine there referred to is of a richer quality than is found in New York or New England.

Since I left Washington in 1873, instead of an

INTRODUCTION

iron wall in front of my desk, I have had a large
window that overlooks the Hudson and the wooded
heights beyond, and I have exchanged the vault for
a vineyard. Probably my mind reacted more vigorously from the former than it does from the latter.
The vineyard winds its tendrils around me and
detains me, and its loaded trellises are more pleasing to me than the closets of greenbacks.

The only time there is a suggestion of an iron
wall in front of me is in winter, when ice and snow
have blotted out the landscape, and I find that it
is in this season that my mind dwells most fondly
upon my favorite themes. Winter drives a man
back upon himself, and tests his powers of self-enter-
tainment.

Do such books as mine give a wrong impression
of Nature, and lead readers to expect more from a
walk or a camp in the woods than they usually get?
I have a few times had occasion to think so. I am
not always aware myself how much pleasure I have
had in a walk till I try to share it with my reader.
The heat of composition brings out the color and
the flavor. We must not forget the illusions of all
art. If my reader thinks he does not get from Nature what I get from her, let me remind him that
he can hardly know what he has got till he defines
it to himself as I do, and throws about it the witch-
ery of words. Literature does not grow wild in
the woods. Every artist does something more than

copy Nature; more comes out in his account than goes into the original experience.

Most persons think the bee gets honey from the flowers, but she does not: honey is a product of the bee; it is the nectar of the flowers with the bee added. What the bee gets from the flower is sweet water: this she puts through a process of her own and imparts to it her own quality; she reduces the water and adds to it a minute drop of formic acid. It is this drop of herself that gives the delicious sting to her sweet. The bee is therefore the type of the true poet, the true artist. Her product always reflects her environment, and it reflects something her environment knows not of. We taste the clover, the thyme, the linden, the sumac, and we also taste something that has its source in none of these flowers.

The literary naturalist does not take liberties with facts; facts are the flora upon which he lives. The more and the fresher the facts the better. I can do nothing without them, but I must give them my own flavor. I must impart to them a quality which heightens and intensifies them.

To interpret Nature is not to improve upon her: it is to draw her out ; it is to have an emotional intercourse with her, absorb her, and reproduce her tinged with the colors of the spirit.

If I name every bird I see in my walk, describe its color and ways, etc., give a lot of facts or details

INTRODUCTION

about the bird, it is doubtful if my reader is interested. But if I relate the bird in some way to human life, to my own life, — show what it is to me and what it is in the landscape and the season, — then do I give my reader a live bird and not a labeled specimen.

J. B.

1895.

WAKE–ROBIN

WAKE-ROBIN

I

THE RETURN OF THE BIRDS

SPRING in our northern climate may fairly be
said to extend from the middle of March to
the middle of June. At least, the vernal tide continues to rise until the latter date, and it is not till
after the summer solstice that the shoots and
twigs begin to harden and turn to wood, or the
grass to lose any of its freshness and succulency.

It is this period that marks the return of the
birds, — one or two of the more hardy or half-
domesticated species, like the song sparrow and
the bluebird, usually arriving in March, while the
rarer and more brilliant wood-birds bring up the
procession in June. But each stage of the advan-
cing season gives prominence to certain species, as
to certain flowers. The dandelion tells me when to
look for the swallow, the dogtooth violet when to
expect the wood-thrush, and when I have found the
wake-robin in bloom I know the season is fairly
inaugurated. With me this flower is associated, not
merely with the awakening of Robin, for he has

3

been awake some weeks, but with the universal awakening and rehabilitation of nature.

Yet the coming and going of the birds is more or less a mystery and a surprise. We go out in the morning, and no thrush or vireo is to be heard ; we go out again, and every tree and grove is musical; yet again, and all is silent. Who saw them come? Who saw them depart?

This pert little winter wren, for instance, darting in and out the fence, diving under the rubbish here and coming up yards away, — how does he manage with those little circular wings to compass degrees and zones, and arrive always in the nick of time? Last August I saw him in the remotest wilds of the Adirondacks, impatient and inquisitive as usual ; a few weeks later, on the Potomac, I was greeted by the same hardy little busybody. Does he travel by easy stages from bush to bush and from wood to wood? or has that compact little body force and courage to brave the night and the upper air, and so achieve leagues at one pull?

And yonder bluebird with the earth tinge on his breast and the sky tinge on his back, — did he come down out of heaven on that bright March morning when he told us so softly and plaintively that, if we pleased, spring had come? Indeed, there is nothing in the return of the birds more curious and suggestive than in the first appearance,

4

or rumors of the appearance, of this little blue-coat. The bird at first seems a mere wandering voice in the air : one hears its call or carol on some bright March morning, but is uncertain of its source or direction ; it falls like a drop of rain when no cloud is visible ; one looks and listens, but to no purpose. The weather changes, perhaps a cold snap with snow comes on, and it may be a week before I hear the note again, and this time or the next perchance see the bird sitting on a stake in the fence lifting his wing as he calls cheerily to his mate. Its notes now become daily more frequent; the birds multiply, and, flitting from point to point, call and warble more confidently and gleefully. Their boldness increases till one sees them hovering with a saucy, inquiring air about barns and out-buildings, peeping into dove-cotes and stable windows, inspecting knotholes and pump-trees, intent only on a place to nest. They wage war against robins and wrens, pick quarrels with swallows, and seem to deliberate for days over the policy of taking forcible possession of one of the mud-houses of the latter. But as the season advances they drift more into the background. Schemes of conquest which they at first seemed bent upon are abandoned, and they settle down very quietly in their old quarters in remote stumpy fields.

Not long after the bluebird comes the robin, sometimes in March, but in most of the Northern

States April is the month of the robin. In large numbers they scour the fields and groves. You hear their piping in the meadow, in the pasture, on the hillside. Walk in the woods, and the dry leaves rustle with the whir of their wings, the air is vocal with their cheery call. In excess of joy and vivacity, they run, leap, scream, chase each other through the air, diving and sweeping among the trees with perilous rapidity.

In that free, fascinating, half-work and half-play pursuit, — sugar-making, — a pursuit which still lingers in many parts of New York, as in New England, — the robin is one's constant companion. When the day is sunny and the ground bare, you meet him at all points and hear him at all hours. At sunset, on the tops of the tall maples, with look heavenward, and in a spirit of utter abandonment, he carols his simple strain. And sitting thus amid the stark, silent trees, above the wet, cold earth, with the chill of winter still in the air, there is no fitter or sweeter songster in the whole round year. It is in keeping with the scene and the occasion. How round and genuine the notes are, and how eagerly our ears drink them in! The first utterance, and the spell of winter is thoroughly broken, and the remembrance of it afar off.

Robin is one of the most native and democratic of our birds; he is one of the family, and seems much nearer to us than those rare, exotic visitants,

6

as the orchard starling or rose-breasted grosbeak, with their distant, high-bred ways. Hardy, noisy, frolicsome, neighborly, and domestic in his habits, strong of wing and bold in spirit, he is the pioneer of the thrush family, and well worthy of the finer artists whose coming he heralds and in a measure prepares us for.

I could wish Robin less native and plebeian in one respect, — the building of his nest. Its coarse material and rough masonry are creditable neither to his skill as a workman nor to his taste as an artist. I am the more forcibly reminded of his deficiency in this respect from observing yonder hummingbird's nest, which is a marvel of fitness and adaptation, a proper setting for this winged gem, — the body of it composed of a white, felt-like substance, probably the down of some plant or the wool of some worm, and toned down in keeping with the branch on which it sits by minute tree-lichens, woven together by threads as fine and frail as gossamer. From Robin's good looks and musical turn, we might reasonably predict a domicile of equal fitness and elegance. At least I demand of him as clean and handsome a nest as the kingbird's, whose harsh jingle, compared with Robin's evening melody, is as the clatter of pots and kettles beside the tone of a flute. I love his note and ways better even than those of the orchard starling or the Baltimore oriole; yet his nest, compared with theirs, is a half-subterranean hut contrasted with a Roman villa. There is something courtly and poetical in a pensile nest. Next to a castle in the air is a dwelling suspended to the slender branch of a tall tree, swayed and rocked forever by the wind. Why need wings be afraid of falling? Why build only where boys can climb? After all, we must set it down to the account of Robin's democratic turn : he is no aristocrat, but one of the people ; and therefore we should expect stability in his workmanship, rather than elegance.

Another April bird, which makes her appearance sometimes earlier and sometimes later than Robin, and whose memory I fondly cherish, is the phœbe-bird, the pioneer of the flycatchers. In the inland farming districts, I used to notice her, on some bright morning about Easter Day, proclaiming her arrival, with much variety of motion and attitude, from the peak of the barn or hay-shed. As yet, you may have heard only the plaintive, homesick note of the bluebird, or the faint trill of the song sparrow; and Phœbe's clear, vivacious assurance of her veritable bodily presence among us again is welcomed by all ears. At agreeable intervals in her lay she describes a circle or an ellipse in the air, ostensibly prospecting for insects, but really, I suspect, as an artistic flourish, thrown in to make up in some way for the deficiency of her musical performance. If plainness of dress indicates powers of song, as it usually does, then Phœbe ought to be unrivaled in musical ability, for surely that ashen-gray suit is the superlative of plainness ; and that form, likewise, would hardly pass for a "perfect figure" of a bird. The seasonableness of her coming, however, and her civil, neighborly ways, shall make up for all deficiencies in song and plumage. After a few weeks Phœbe is seldom seen, except as she darts from her moss-covered nest beneath some bridge or shelving cliff.

Another April comer, who arrives shortly after Robin-redbreast, with whom he associates both at this season and in the autumn, is the gold-winged woodpecker, *alias* "high-hole," *alias* "flicker," *alias* "yarup." He is an old favorite of my boyhood, and his note to me means very much. He announces his arrival by a long, loud call, repeated from the dry branch of some tree, or a stake in the fence, — a thoroughly melodious April sound. I think how Solomon finished that beautiful description of spring, "And the voice of the turtle is heard in the land," and see that a description of spring in this farming country, to be equally characteristic, should culminate in like manner, — "And the call of the high-hole comes up from the wood."

It is a loud, strong, sonorous call, and does not seem to imply an answer, but rather to subserve some purpose of love or music. It is "Yarup's" proclamation of peace and good-will to all. On looking at the matter closely, I perceive that most birds. not denominated songsters, have, in the spring, some note or sound or call that hints of a song, and answers imperfectly the end of beauty and art. As a "livelier iris changes on the burnished dove," and the fancy of the young man turns lightly to thoughts of his pretty cousin, so the same renewing spirit touches the "silent singers," and they are no longer dumb; faintly they lisp the first syllables of the marvelous tale. Witness the clear, sweet whistle of the gray-crested titmouse, — the soft, nasal piping of the nuthatch, — the amorous, vivacious warble of the bluebird, — the long, rich note of the meadowlark, — the whistle of the quail, — the drumming of the partridge, — the animation and loquacity of the swallows, and the like. Even the hen has a homely, contented carol; and I credit the owls with a desire to fill the night with music. All birds are incipient or would-be songsters in the spring. I find corroborative evidence of this even in the crowing of the cock. The flowering of the maple is not so obvious as that of the magnolia; nevertheless, there is actual inflorescence.

Few writers award any song to that familiar little sparrow. the *Socialis ;* yet who that has observed him sitting by the wayside, and repeating, with devout attitude, that fine sliding chant, does not recognize the neglect? Who has heard the snowbird sing? Yet he has a lisping warble very savory to the ear. I have heard him indulge in it even in February.

Even the cow bunting feels the musical tendency, and aspires to its expression, with the rest. Perched upon the topmost branch beside his mate or mates, — for he is quite a polygamist, and usually has two or three demure little ladies in faded black beside him, — generally in the early part of the day, he seems literally to vomit up his notes. Apparently with much labor and effort, they gurgle and blubber up out of him, falling on the ear with a peculiar subtile ring, as of turning water from a glass bottle, and not without a certain pleasing cadence.

Neither is the common woodpecker entirely insensible to the wooing of the spring, and, like the partridge, testifies his appreciation of melody after quite a primitive fashion. Passing through the woods on some clear, still morning in March, while the metallic ring and tension of winter are still in the earth and air, the silence is suddenly broken by long, resonant hammering upon a dry limb or stub. It is Downy beating a reveille to spring. In the utter stillness and amid the rigid forms we listen with pleasure; and, as it comes to my ear oftener at this season than at any other, I freely exonerate the author of it from the imputation of any gas-

11

tronomic motives, and credit him with a genuine musical performance.

It is to be expected, therefore, that "yellow-hammer" will respond to the general tendency, and contribute his part to the spring chorus. His April call is his finest touch, his most musical expression.

I recall an ancient maple standing sentry to a large sugar-bush, that, year after year, afforded protection to a brood of yellow-hammers in its decayed heart. A week or two before the nesting seemed actually to have begun, three or four of these birds might be seen, on almost any bright morning, gamboling and courting amid its decayed branches. Sometimes you would hear only a gentle persuasive cooing, or a quiet confidential chattering, — then that long, loud call, taken up by first one, then another, as they sat about upon the naked limbs, — anon, a sort of wild, rollicking laughter, intermingled with various cries, yelps, and squeals, as if some incident had excited their mirth and ridicule. Whether this social hilarity and boisterousness is in celebration of the pairing or mating ceremony, or whether it is only a sort of annual "house-warming" common among high-holes on resuming their summer quarters, is a question upon which I reserve my judgment.

Unlike most of his kinsmen, the golden-wing prefers the fields and the borders of the forest to the deeper seclusion of the woods, and hence, contrary to the habit of his tribe, obtains most of his subsistence from the ground, probing it for ants and crickets. He is not quite satisfied with being a woodpecker. He courts the society of the robin and the finches, abandons the trees for the meadow, and feeds eagerly upon berries and grain. What may be the final upshot of this course of living is a question worthy the attention of Darwin. Will his taking to the ground and his pedestrian feats result in lengthening his legs, his feeding upon berries and grains subdue his tints and soften his voice, and his associating with Robin put a song into his heart?

Indeed, what would be more interesting than the history of our birds for the last two or three centuries? There can be no doubt that the presence of man has exerted a very marked and friendly influence upon them, since they so multiply in his society. The birds of California, it is said, were mostly silent till after its settlement, and I doubt if the Indians heard the wood thrush as we hear him. Where did the bobolink disport himself before there were meadows in the North and rice-fields in the South? Was he the same lithe, merry-hearted beau then as now? And the sparrow, the lark, and the goldfinch, birds that seem so indigenous to the open fields and so averse to the woods, — we cannot conceive of their existence in a vast wilderness and without man.

But to return. The song sparrow, that universal favorite and firstling of the spring, comes before April, and its simple strain gladdens all hearts.

May is the month of the swallows and the orioles. There are many other distinguished arrivals, indeed nine tenths of the birds are here by the last week in May, yet the swallows and orioles are the most conspicuous. The bright plumage of the latter seems really like an arrival from the tropics. I see them dash through the blossoming trees, and all the forenoon hear their incessant warbling and wooing. The swallows dive and chatter about the barn, or squeak and build beneath the eaves; the partridge drums in the fresh sprouting woods; the long, tender note of the meadowlark comes up from the meadow; and at sunset, from every marsh and pond come the ten thousand voices of the hylas. May is the transition month, and exists to connect April and June, the root with the flower.

With June the cup is full, our hearts are satisfied, there is no more to be desired. The perfection of the season, among other things, has brought the perfection of the song and plumage of the birds. The master artists are all here ; and the expectations excited by the robin and the song sparrow are fully justified. The thrushes have all come ; and I sit down upon the first rock, with hands full of the pink azalea, to listen. With me, the cuckoo does not arrive till June ; and often the goldfinch, the kingbird, the scarlet tanager delay their coming till then. In the meadows the bobolink is in all his glory; in the high pastures the field sparrow sings his breezy vesper-hymn ; and the woods are unfolding to the music of the thrushes.

The cuckoo is one of the most solitary birds of our forests, and is strangely tame and quiet, appearing equally untouched by joy or grief, fear or anger. Something remote seems ever weighing upon his mind. His note or call is as of one lost or wandering, and to the farmer is prophetic of rain. Amid the general joy and the sweet assurance of things, I love to listen to the strange clairvoyant call. Heard a quarter of a mile away, from out the depths of the forest, there is something peculiarly weird and monkish about it. Wordsworth's lines upon the European species apply equally well to ours: —

"O blithe new-comer ! I have heard,
    I hear thee and rejoice:
O cuckoo! shall I call thee bird?
    Or but a wandering voice?

"While I am lying on the grass,
    Thy loud note smites my ear !
From hill to hill it seems to pass,
    At once far off and near !

15

"Thrice welcome, darling of the spring !
Even yet thou art to me
No bird, but an invisible thing,
A voice, a mystery."

The black-billed is the only species found in my locality, the yellow-billed abounds farther south. Their note or call is nearly the same. The former sometimes suggests the voice of a turkey. The call of the latter may be suggested thus: *k-k-k-k-k-kow*, *kow*, *kow-ow*, *kow-ow*.

The yellow-billed will take up his stand in a tree, and explore its branches till he has caught every worm. He sits on a twig, and with a peculiar swaying movement of his head examines the surrounding foliage. When he discovers his prey, he leaps upon it in a fluttering manner.

In June the black-billed makes a tour through the orchard and garden, regaling himself upon the canker-worms. At this time he is one of the tamest of birds, and will allow you to approach within a few yards of him. I have even come within a few feet of one without seeming to excite his fear or suspicion. He is quite unsophisticated, or else royally indifferent.

The plumage of the cuckoo is a rich glossy brown, and is unrivaled in beauty by any other neutral tint with which I am acquainted. It is also remarkable for its firmness and fineness.

Notwithstanding the disparity in size and color,

16

the black-billed species has certain peculiarities
that remind one of the passenger pigeon. His eye,
with its red circle, the shape of his head, and his
motions on alighting and taking flight, quickly suggest the resemblance; though in grace and speed,
when on the wing, he is far inferior. His tail seems
disproportionately long, like that of the red thrush,
and his flight among the trees is very still, contrasting strongly with the honest clatter of the robin
or pigeon.

Have you heard the song of the field sparrow?
If you have lived in a pastoral country with broad
upland pastures, you could hardly have missed
him. Wilson, I believe, calls him the grass finch,
and was evidently unacquainted with his powers of
song. The two white lateral quills in his tail, and
his habit of running and skulking a few yards in
advance of you as you walk through the fields, are
sufficient to identify him. Not in meadows or
orchards, but in high, breezy pasture-grounds, will
you look for him. His song is most noticeable
after sundown, when other birds are silent; for
which reason he has been aptly called the vesper
sparrow. The farmer following his team from the
field at dusk catches his sweetest strain. His song
is not so brisk and varied as that of the song sparrow, being softer and wilder, sweeter and more
plaintive. Add the best parts of the lay of the latter
to the sweet vibrating chant of the wood sparrow,

and you have the evening hymn of the vesper-bird, — the poet of the plain, unadorned pastures. Go to those broad, smooth, uplying fields where the cattle and sheep are grazing, and sit down in the twilight on one of those warm, clean stones, and listen to this song. On every side, near and remote, from out the short grass which the herds are cropping, the strain rises. Two or three long, silver notes of peace and rest, ending in some subdued trills and quavers, constitute each separate song. Often you will catch only one or two of the bars, the breeze having blown the minor part away. Such unambitious, quiet, unconscious melody! It is one of the most characteristic sounds in nature. The grass, the stones, the stubble, the furrow, the quiet herds, and the warm twilight among the hills, are all subtly expressed in this song; this is what they are at last capable of.

The female builds a plain nest in the open field, without so much as a bush or thistle or tuft of grass to protect it or mark its site; you may step upon it, or the cattle may tread it into the ground. But the danger from this source, I presume, the bird considers less than that from another. Skunks and foxes have a very impertinent curiosity, as Finchie well knows; and a bank or hedge, or a rank growth of grass or thistles, that might promise protection and cover to mouse or bird, these cunning rogues would be apt to explore most thoroughly. The partridge is undoubtedly acquainted with the same process of reasoning ; for, like the vesper-bird, she, too, nests in open, unprotected places, avoiding all show of concealment, — coming from the tangled and almost impenetrable parts of the forest to the clean, open woods, where she can command all the approaches and fly with equal ease in any direction.

Another favorite sparrow, but little noticed. is the wood or bush sparrow, usually called by the ornithologists *Spizella pusilla*. Its size and form is that of the *socialis*, but is less distinctly marked, being of a duller redder tinge. He prefers remote bushy heathery fields, where his song is one of the sweetest to be heard. It is sometimes very notice-able, especially early in spring. I remember sit-ting one bright day in the still leafless April woods, when one of these birds struck up a few rods from me, repeating its lay at short intervals for nearly an hour. It was a perfect piece of wood-music, and was of course all the more noticeable for being projected upon such a broad unoccupied page of silence. Its song is like the words, *fe-o, fe-o, fe-o, few, few, few, fee fee fee*, uttered at first high and leisurely, but running very rapidly toward the close, which is low and soft.

Still keeping among the unrecognized, the white-eyed vireo, or flycatcher, deserves particular men-tion. The song of this bird is not particularly sweet and soft ; on the contrary, it is a little hard and shrill, like that of the indigo-bird or oriole ; but for brightness, volubility, execution, and power of imitation, he is unsurpassed by any of our northern birds. His ordinary note is forcible and emphatic, but, as stated, not especially musical; *Chick-a-re'r-chick*, he seems to say, hiding himself in the low, dense undergrowth, and eluding your most vigilant search, as if playing some part in a game. But in July or August, if you are on good terms with the sylvan deities, you may listen to a far more rare and artistic performance. Your first impression will be that that cluster of azalea, or that clump of swamp-huckleberry, conceals three or four different songsters, each vying with the others to lead the chorus. Such a medley of notes, snatched from half the songsters of the field and forest, and uttered with the utmost clearness and rapidity, I am sure you cannot hear short of the haunts of the genuine mockingbird. If not fully and accurately repeated, there are at least suggested the notes of the robin, wren, catbird, high-hole, goldfinch, and song sparrow. The *pip, pip*, of the last is produced so accurately that I verily believe it would deceive the bird herself; and the whole uttered in such rapid succession that it seems as if the movement that gives the concluding note of one strain must form the first note of the next. The effect is very rich, and, to my ear, entirely unique. The performer is

20

Partridge's Nest

very careful not to reveal himself in the mean time; yet there is a conscious air about the strain that impresses me with the idea that my presence is understood and my attention courted. A tone of pride and glee, and, occasionally, of bantering jocoseness, is discernible. I believe it is only rarely, and when he is sure of his audience, that he displays his parts in this manner. You are to look for him, not in tall trees or deep forests, but in low, dense shrubbery about wet places, where there are plenty of gnats and mosquitoes.

The winter wren is another marvelous songster, in speaking of whom it is difficult to avoid superlatives. He is not so conscious of his powers and so ambitious of effect as the white-eyed flycatcher, yet you will not be less astonished and delighted on hearing him. He possesses the fluency and copiousness for which the wrens are noted, and besides these qualities, and what is rarely found conjoined with them, a wild, sweet, rhythmical cadence that holds you entranced. I shall not soon forget that perfect June day, when, loitering in a low, ancient hemlock wood, in whose cathedral aisles the coolness and freshness seems perennial, the silence was suddenly broken by a strain so rapid and gushing, and touched with such a wild, sylvan plaintiveness, that I listened in amazement. And so shy and coy was the little minstrel, that I came twice to the woods before I was sure to whom I was listening. In summer he is one of those birds of the deep northern forests, that, like the speckled Canada warbler and the hermit thrush, only the privileged ones hear.

The distribution of plants in a given locality is not more marked and defined than that of the birds. Show a botanist a landscape, and he will tell you where to look for the lady's-slipper, the columbine, or the harebell. On the same principles the ornithologist will direct you where to look for the greenlets, the wood sparrow, or the chewink. In adjoining counties, in the same latitude, and equally inland, but possessing a different geological formation and different forest-timber, you will observe quite a different class of birds. In a land of the beech and sugar maple I do not find the same songsters that I know where thrive the oak, chestnut, and laurel. In going from a district of the Old Red Sandstone to where I walk upon the old Plutonic Rock, not fifty miles distant, I miss in the woods the veery, the hermit thrush, the chestnut-sided warbler, the blue-backed warbler, the green-backed warbler, the black and yellow warbler, and many others, and find in their stead the wood thrush, the chewink, the redstart, the yellow-throat, the yellow-breasted flycatcher, the white-eyed flycatcher, the quail, and the turtle dove.

In my neighborhood here in the Highlands the distribution is very marked. South of the village I invariably find one species of birds, north of it another. In only one locality, full of azalea and swamp-huckleberry, I am always sure of finding the hooded warbler. In a dense undergrowth of spice-bush, witch-hazel, and alder, I meet the worm-eating warbler. In a remote clearing, covered with heath and fern, with here and there a chestnut and an oak, I go to hear in July the wood sparrow, and returning by a stumpy, shallow pond, I am sure to find the water-thrush.

Only one locality within my range seems to pos-sess attractions for all comers. Here one may study almost the entire ornithology of the State. It is a rocky piece of ground, long ago cleared, but now fast relapsing into the wildness and freedom of nature, and marked by those half-cultivated, half-wild features which birds and boys love. It is bounded on two sides by the village and highway, crossed at various points by carriage-roads, and threaded in all directions by paths and byways, along which soldiers, laborers, and truant school-boys are passing at all hours of the day. It is so far escaping from the axe and the bush-hook as to have opened communication with the forest and mountain beyond by straggling lines of cedar, laurel, and blackberry. The ·ground is mainly occupied with cedar and chestnut, with an undergrowth, in many places, of heath and bramble. The chief feature, however, is a dense growth in the centre, consisting of dogwood, water-beech, swamp-ash, alder, spice-bush, hazel, etc., with a network of smilax and frost-grape. A little zigzag stream, the draining of a swamp beyond, which passes through this tanglewood, accounts for many of its features and productions, if not for its entire existence. Birds that are not attracted by the heath, or the cedar and chestnut, are sure to find some excuse for visiting this miscellaneous growth in the centre. Most of the common birds literally throng this idle-wild; and I have met here many of the rarer species, such as the great-crested flycatcher, the solitary warbler, the blue-winged swamp warbler, the worm-eating warbler, the fox sparrow, etc. The absence of all birds of prey, and the great number of flies and insects, both the result of proximity to the village, are considerations which no hawk-fearing, peace-loving minstrel passes over lightly; hence the popularity of the resort.

But the crowning glory of all these robins, fly-catchers, and warblers is the wood thrush. More abundant than all other birds, except the robin and catbird, he greets you from every rock and shrub. Shy and reserved when he first makes his appearance in May, before the end of June he is tame and familiar, and sings on the tree over your head, or on the rock a few paces in advance. A pair even built their nest and reared their brood within ten or twelve feet of the piazza of a large summer-house in the vicinity. But when the guests commenced to arrive and the piazza to be thronged with gay crowds, I noticed something like dread and foreboding in the manner of the mother bird; and from her still, quiet ways, and habit of sitting long and silently within a few feet of the precious charge, it seemed as if the dear creature had resolved, if possible, to avoid all observation.

If we take the quality of melody as the test, the wood thrush, hermit thrush, and the veery thrush stand at the head of our list of songsters.

The mockingbird undoubtedly possesses the greatest range of mere talent, the most varied executive ability, and never fails to surprise and delight one anew at each hearing ; but being mostly an imitator, he never approaches the serene beauty and sublimity of the hermit thrush. The word that best expresses my feelings, on hearing the mockingbird, is admiration, though the first emotion is one of surprise and incredulity. That so many and such various notes should proceed from one throat is a marvel, and we regard the performance with feelings akin to those we experience on witnessing the astounding feats of the athlete or gymnast,— and this, notwithstanding many of the notes imitated have all the freshness and sweetness of the originals. The emotions excited by the songs of these thrushes belong to a higher order, springing as they do from our deepest sense of the beauty and harmony of the world.

The wood thrush is worthy of all, and more than all, the praises he has received; and considering the number of his appreciative listeners, it is not a little surprising that his relative and equal, the hermit thrush, should have received so little notice. Both the great ornithologists, Wilson and Audubon, are lavish in their praises of the former, but have little or nothing to say of the song of the latter. Audubon says it is sometimes agreeable, but evidently has never heard it. Nuttall, I am glad to find, is more discriminating, and does the bird fuller justice.

It is quite a rare bird, of very shy and secluded habits, being found in the Middle and Eastern States, during the period of song, only in the deepest and most remote forests, usually in damp and swampy localities. On this account the people in the Adirondack region call it the "Swamp Angel." Its being so much of a recluse accounts for the comparative ignorance that prevails in regard to it.

The cast of its song is very much like that of the wood thrush, and a good observer might easily confound the two. But hear them together and the difference is quite marked: the song of the hermit is in a higher key, and is more wild and ethereal. His instrument is a silver horn which he winds in the most solitary places. The song of the wood thrush is more golden and leisurely. Its tone comes near to that of some rare stringed instrument. One feels that perhaps the wood thrush has more compass and power, if he would only let himself out, but on the whole he comes a little short of the pure, serene, hymn-like strain of the hermit.

Yet those who have heard only the wood thrush may well place him first on the list. He is truly a royal minstrel, and, considering his liberal distribution throughout our Atlantic seaboard, perhaps contributes more than any other bird to our sylvan melody. One may object that he spends a little too much time in tuning his instrument, yet his careless and uncertain touches reveal its rare compass and power.

He is the only songster of my acquaintance, excepting the canary, that displays different degrees of proficiency in the exercise of his musical gifts. Not long since, while walking one Sunday in the edge of an orchard adjoining a wood, I heard one that so obviously and unmistakably surpassed all his rivals, that my companion, though slow to notice such things, remarked it wonderingly; and with one accord we paused to listen to so rare a performer. It was not different in quality so much as in quantity. Such a flood of it! Such copiousness! Such long, trilling, accelerating preludes! Such sudden, ecstatic overtures would have intoxicated the dullest ear. He was really without a compeer, — a master-artist. Twice afterward I was conscious of having heard the same bird.

The wood thrush is the handsomest species of
this family. In grace and elegance of manner he
has no equal. Such a gentle, high-bred air, and
such inimitable ease and composure in his flight and
movement! He is a poet in very word and deed.
His carriage is music to the eye. His performance
of the commonest act, as catching a beetle, or picking a worm from the mud, pleases like a stroke of
wit or eloquence. Was he a prince in the olden
time, and do the regal grace and mien still adhere
to him in his transformation? What a finely pro-
portioned form! How plain, yet rich, his color,—
the bright russet of his back, the clear white of his
breast, with the distinct heart-shaped spots! It may
be objected to Robin that he is noisy and demonstrative; he hurries away or rises to a branch with
an angry note, and flirts his wings in ill-bred suspicion. The mavis, or red thrush, sneaks and skulks
like a culprit, hiding in the densest alders; the catbird is a coquette and a flirt, as well as a sort of
female Paul Pry; and the chewink shows his in-
hospitality by espying your movements like a Jap-
anese. The wood thrush has none of these under-
bred traits. He regards me unsuspiciously, or avoids
me with a noble reserve,— or, if I am quiet and
incurious, graciously hops toward me, as if to pay
his respects, or to make my acquaintance. I have
passed under his nest within a few feet of his mate
and brood, when he sat near by on a branch eying

me sharply, but without opening his beak ; but the moment I raised my hand toward his defenseless household his anger and indignation were beautiful to behold.

What a noble pride he has! Late one October, after his mates and companions had long since gone south, I noticed one for several successive days in the dense part of this next-door wood, flitting noiselessly about, very grave and silent, as if doing penance for some violation of the code of honor. By many gentle, indirect approaches, I perceived that part of his tail-feathers were undeveloped. The sylvan prince could not think of returning to court in this plight, and so, amid the falling leaves and cold rains of autumn, was patiently biding his time.

The soft, mellow flute of the veery fills a place in the chorus of the woods that the song of the vesper sparrow fills in the chorus of the fields. It has the nightingale's habit of singing in the twilight, as indeed have all our thrushes. Walk out toward the forest in the warm twilight of a June day, and when fifty rods distant you will hear their soft, reverberating notes rising from a dozen different throats.

It is one of the simplest strains to be heard,— as simple as the curve in form, delighting from the pure element of harmony and beauty it contains, and not from any novel or fantastic modulation of it,— thus contrasting strongly with such rollicking, hilarious songsters as the bobolink, in whom we are chiefly pleased with the tintinnabulation, the verbal and labial excellence, and the evident conceit and delight of the performer.

I hardly know whether I am more pleased or annoyed with the catbird. Perhaps she is a little too common, and her part in the general chorus a little too conspicuous. If you are listening for the note of another bird, she is sure to be prompted to the most loud and protracted singing, drowning all other sounds; if you sit quietly down to observe a favorite or study a new-comer, her curiosity knows no bounds, and you are scanned and ridiculed from every point of observation. Yet I would not miss her ; I would only subordinate her a little, make her less conspicuous.

She is the parodist of the woods, and there is ever a mischievous, bantering, half-ironical undertone in her lay, as if she were conscious of mimicking and disconcerting some envied songster. Ambitious of song, practicing and rehearsing in private, she yet seems the least sincere and genuine of the sylvan minstrels, as if she had taken up music only to be in the fashion, or not to be outdone by the robins and thrushes. In other words, she seems to sing from some outward motive, and not from inward joyousness. She is a good versifier, but not a great poet. Vigorous, rapid, copious, not without fine touches, but destitute of any high, serene melody, her performance, like that of Thoreau's squirrel, always implies a spectator.

There is a certain air and polish about her strain, however, like that in the vivacious conversation of a well-bred lady of the world, that commands respect. Her maternal instinct, also, is very strong, and that simple structure of dead twigs and dry grass is the centre of much anxious solicitude. Not long since, while strolling through the woods, my attention was attracted to a small densely grown swamp, hedged in with eglantine, brambles, and the everlasting smilax, from which proceeded loud cries of distress and alarm, indicating that some terrible calamity was threatening my sombre-colored minstrel. On effecting an entrance, which, however, was not accomplished till I had doffed coat and hat, so as to diminish the surface exposed to the thorns and brambles, and, looking around me from a square yard of terra firma, I found myself the spectator of a loathsome yet fascinating scene. Three or four yards from me was the nest, beneath which, in long festoons, rested a huge black snake; a bird two thirds grown was slowly disappearing between his expanded jaws. As he seemed unconscious of my presence, I quietly observed the proceedings. By slow degrees he compassed the bird about with his elastic mouth ; his head flattened, his neck writhed and swelled, and two or three undulatory movements of his glistening body finished the work. Then he cautiously raised himself up, his tongue flaming from his mouth the while, curved over the nest, and, with wavy, subtle motions, explored the interior. I can conceive of nothing more overpoweringly terrible to an unsuspecting family of birds than the sudden appearance above their domicile of the head and neck of this arch-enemy. It is enough to petrify the blood in their veins. Not finding the object of his search, he came streaming down from the nest to a lower limb, and commenced extending his researches in other directions, sliding stealthily through the branches, bent on capturing one of the parent birds. That a legless, wingless creature should move with such ease and rapidity where only birds and squirrels are considered at home, lifting himself up, letting himself down, running out on the yielding boughs, and traversing with marvelous celerity the whole length and breadth of the thicket, was truly surprising. One thinks of the great myth of the Tempter and the " cause of all our woe," and wonders if the Arch One is not now playing off some of his pranks before him. Whether we call it snake or devil matters little. I could but admire his terrible beauty, however; his black, shining folds, his easy, gliding movement, head erect, eyes glistening, tongue playing like subtle flame, and the invisible means of his almost winged locomotion.

The parent birds, in the mean while, kept up the most agonizing cry,— at times fluttering furiously about their pursuer, and actually laying hold of his tail with their beaks and claws. On being thus attacked, the snake would suddenly double upon himself and follow his own body back, thus executing a strategic movement that at first seemed almost to paralyze his victim and place her within his grasp. Not quite, however. Before his jaws could close upon the coveted prize the bird would tear herself away, and, apparently faint and sobbing, retire to a higher branch. His reputed powers of fascination availed him little, though it is possible that a frailer and less combative bird might have been held by the fatal spell. Presently, as he came gliding down the slender body of a leaning alder, his attention was attracted by a slight movement of my arm; eyeing me an instant, with that crouching, utter, motionless gaze which I believe only snakes and devils can assume, he turned quickly,— a feat which necessitated something like crawling over his own body,— and glided off through the branches, evidently recognizing in me a representative of the ancient parties he once so cunningly ruined. A few moments after, as he lay carelessly disposed in the top of a rank alder, trying to look as much like a crooked branch as his supple, shining form would admit, the old vengeance overtook him. I exercised my prerogative, and a well-directed missile, in the shape of a stone, brought him looping and writhing to the ground. After I had completed his downfall and quiet had been partially restored, a half-fledged member of the bereaved household came out from his hiding-place, and, jumping upon a decayed branch, chirped vigorously, no doubt in celebration of the victory.

Till the middle of July there is a general equilibrium; the tide stands poised; the holiday spirit is unabated. But as the harvest ripens beneath the long, hot days, the melody gradually ceases. The young are out of the nest and must be cared for, and the moulting season is at hand. After the cricket has commenced to drone his monotonous refrain beneath your window, you will not, till another season, hear the wood thrush in all his matchless eloquence. The bobolink has become careworn and fretful, and blurts out snatches of his song between his scolding and upbraiding, as you approach the vicinity of his nest, oscillating between anxiety for his brood and solicitude for his musical reputation. Some of the sparrows still sing, and occasionally across the hot fields, from a tall tree in the edge of the forest, comes the rich note of the scarlet tanager. This tropical-colored bird loves the hottest weather, and I hear him even in dog-days.

The remainder of the summer is the carnival of the swallows and flycatchers. Flies and insects,

to any amount, are to be had for the catching;
and the opportunity is well improved. See that
sombre, ashen-colored pewee on yonder branch.
A true sportsman he, who never takes his game
at rest, but always on the wing. You vagrant
fly, you purblind moth, beware how you come
within his range! Observe his attitude, the curious
movement of his head, his "eye in a fine frenzy
rolling, glancing from heaven to earth, from earth
to heaven."

His sight is microscopic and his aim sure. Quick
as thought he has seized his victim and is back to
his perch. There is no strife, no pursuit,— one
fell swoop and the matter is ended. That little
sparrow, as you will observe, is less skilled. It is
the *Socialis*, and he finds his subsistence properly
in various seeds and the larvæ of insects, though
he occasionally has higher aspirations, and seeks
to emulate the pewee, commencing and ending
his career 'as a flycatcher by an awkward chase
after a beetle or "miller." He is hunting around
in the grass now, I suspect, with the desire to indulge this favorite whim. There! — the opportunity is afforded him. Away goes a little cream-
colored meadow-moth in the most tortuous course
he is capable of, and away goes *Socialis* in pursuit.
The contest is quite comical, though I dare say it
is serious enough to the moth. The chase continues for a few yards, when there is a sudden rush-

ing to cover in the grass,— then a taking to wing again, when the search has become too close, and the moth has recovered his wind. *Socialis* chirps angrily, and is determined not to be beaten. Keeping, with the slightest effort, upon the heels of the fugitive, he is ever on the point of halting to snap him up, but never quite does it,— and so, between disappointment and expectation, is soon disgusted, and returns to pursue his more legitimate means of subsistence.

In striking contrast to this serio-comic strife of the sparrow and the moth, is the pigeon hawk's pursuit of the sparrow or the goldfinch. It is a race of surprising speed and agility. It is a test of wing and wind. Every muscle is taxed, and every nerve strained. Such cries of terror and consternation on the part of the bird, tacking to the right and left, and making the most desperate efforts to escape, and such silent determination on the part of the hawk, pressing the bird so closely, flashing and turning, and timing his movements with those of the pursued as accurately and as inexorably as if the two constituted one body, excite feelings of the deepest concern. You mount the fence or rush out of your way to see the issue. The only salvation for the bird is to adopt the tactics of the moth, seeking instantly the cover of some tree, bush, or hedge, where its smaller size enables it to move about more rapidly. These pirates are aware of this, and there-

fore prefer to take their prey by one fell swoop.
You may see one of them prowling through an
orchard, with the yellowbirds hovering about him,
crying, *Pi-ty, pi-ty*, in the most desponding tone ;
yet he seems not to regard them, knowing, as do
they, that in the close branches they are as safe
as if in a wall of adamant.

August is the month of the high-sailing hawks.
The hen-hawk is the most noticeable. He likes
the haze and calm of these long, warm days. He
is a bird of leisure, and seems always at his ease.
How beautiful and majestic are his movements!
So self-poised and easy, such an entire absence of
haste, such a magnificent amplitude of circles and
spirals, such a haughty, imperial grace, and, occasionally, such daring aerial evolutions!

With slow, leisurely movement, rarely vibrating
his pinions, he mounts and mounts in an ascending
spiral till he appears a mere speck against the summer sky; then, if the mood seizes him, with wings
half-closed, like a bent bow, he will cleave the air
almost perpendicularly, as if intent on dashing
himself to pieces against the earth; but on nearing
the ground he suddenly mounts again on broad, expanded wing, as if rebounding upon the air, and sails
leisurely away. It is the sublimest feat of the season.
One holds his breath till he sees him rise again.

If inclined to a more gradual and less precipitous descent, he fixes his eye on some distant point

in the earth beneath him, and thither bends his course. He is still almost meteoric in his speed and boldness. You see his path down the heavens, straight as a line; if near, you hear the rush of his wings; his shadow hurtles across the fields, and in an instant you see him quietly perched upon some low tree or decayed stub in a swamp or meadow, with reminiscences of frogs and mice stirring in his maw.

When the south wind blows, it is a study to see three or four of these air-kings at the head of the valley far up toward the mountain, balancing and oscillating upon the strong current; now quite stationary, except a slight tremulous motion like the poise of a rope-dancer, then rising and falling in long undulations, and seeming to resign themselves passively to the wind ; or, again, sailing high and level far above the mountain's peak, no bluster and haste, but, as stated, occasionally a terrible earnestness and speed. Fire at one as he sails overhead, and, unless wounded badly, he will not change his course or gait.

His flight is a perfect picture of repose in motion. It strikes the eye as more surprising than the flight of the pigeon and swallow even, in that the effort put forth is so uniform and delicate as to escape observation, giving to the movement an air of buoyancy and perpetuity, the effluence of power rather than the conscious application of it.

THE RETURN OF THE BIRDS

The calmness and dignity of this hawk, when attacked by crows or the kingbird, are well worthy of him. He seldom deigns to notice his noisy and furious antagonists, but deliberately wheels about in that aerial spiral, and mounts and mounts till his pursuers grow dizzy and return to earth again. It is quite original, this mode of getting rid of an unworthy opponent, rising to heights where the braggart is dazed and bewildered and loses his reckoning! I am not sure but it is worthy of imitation.

But summer wanes, and autumn approaches. The songsters of the seed-time are silent at the reaping of the harvest. Other minstrels take up the strain. It is the heyday of insect life. The day is canopied with musical sound. All the songs of the spring and summer appear to be floating, softened and refined, in the upper air. The birds, in a new but less holiday suit, turn their faces southward. The swallows flock and go ; the bobolinks flock and go; silently and unobserved, the thrushes go. Autumn arrives, bringing finches, warblers, sparrows, and kinglets from the north. Silently the procession passes. Yonder hawk, sailing peacefully away till he is lost in the horizon, is a symbol of the closing season and the departing birds.

1863.

II

IN THE HEMLOCKS

MOST people receive with incredulity a statement of the number of birds that annually visit our climate. Very few even are aware of half the number that spend the summer in their own immediate vicinity. We little suspect, when we walk in the woods, whose privacy we are intruding upon, — what rare and elegant visitants from Mexico, from Central and South America, and from the islands of the sea, are holding their reunions in the branches over our heads, or pursuing their pleasure on the ground before us.

I recall the altogether admirable and shining family which Thoreau dreamed he saw in the upper chambers of Spaulding's woods, which Spaulding did not know lived there, and which were not put out when Spaulding, whistling, drove his team through their lower halls. They did not go into society in the village; they were quite well; they had sons and daughters; they neither wove nor spun; there was a sound as of suppressed hilarity.

I take it for granted that the forester was only saying a pretty thing of the birds, though I have observed that it does sometimes annoy them when Spaulding's cart rumbles through their house. Generally, however, they are as unconscious of Spaulding as Spaulding is of them.

Walking the other day in an old hemlock wood, I counted over forty varieties of these summer visitants, many of them common to other woods in the vicinity, but quite a number peculiar to these ancient solitudes, and not a few that are rare in any locality. It is quite unusual to find so large a number abiding in one forest, — and that not a large one, — most of them nesting and spending the summer there. Many of those I observed commonly pass this season much farther north. But the geographical distribution of birds is rather a climatical one. The same temperature, though under different parallels, usually attracts the same birds; difference in altitude being equivalent to the difference in latitude. A given height above the sea-level under the parallel of thirty degrees may have the same climate as places under that of thirty-five degrees, and similar flora and fauna. At the headwaters of the Delaware, where I write, the latitude is that of Boston, but the region has a much greater elevation, and hence a climate that compares better with the northern part of the State and of New England. Half a day's drive to the southeast brings me down into quite a different temperature, with an older geological formation, different forest timber, and different birds, — even with different mammals. Neither the little gray rabbit nor the little gray fox is found in my locality, but the great northern hare and the red fox are. In the last century a colony of beavers dwelt here, though the oldest inhabitant cannot now point to even the traditional site of their dams. The ancient hemlocks, whither I propose to take the reader, are rich in many things besides birds. Indeed, their wealth in this respect is owing mainly, no doubt, to their rank vegetable growths, their fruitful swamps, and their dark, sheltered retreats.

Their history is of an heroic cast. Ravished and torn by the tanner in his thirst for bark, preyed upon by the lumberman, assaulted and beaten back by the settler, still their spirit has never been broken, their energies never paralyzed. Not many years ago a public highway passed through them, but it was at no time a tolerable road; trees fell across it, mud and limbs choked it up, till finally travelers took the hint and went around; and now, walking along its deserted course, I see only the footprints of coons, foxes, and squirrels.

Nature loves such woods, and places her own seal upon them. Here she shows me what can be done with ferns and mosses and lichens. The soil is marrowy and full of innumerable forests. Standing in these fragrant aisles, I feel the strength of the vegetable kingdom, and am awed by the deep and inscrutable processes of life going on so silently about me.

No hostile forms with axe or spud now visit these solitudes. The cows have half-hidden ways through them, and know where the best browsing is to be had. In spring, the farmer repairs to their bordering of maples to make sugar; in July and August, women and boys from all the country about penetrate the old Barkpeelings for raspberries and blackberries; and I know a youth who wonderingly follows their languid stream casting for trout.

In like spirit, alert and buoyant, on this bright June morning go I also to reap my harvest, — pursuing a sweet more delectable than sugar, fruit more savory than berries, and game for another palate than that tickled by trout.

June, of all the months, the student of ornithology can least afford to lose. Most birds are nesting then, and in full song and plumage. And what is a bird without its song? Do we not wait for the stranger to speak? It seems to me that I do not know a bird till I have heard its voice; then I come nearer it at once, and it possesses a human interest to me. I have met the gray-cheeked thrush in the woods, and held him in my hand; still I do not know him. The silence of the cedar-bird throws a mystery about him which neither his good looks nor his petty larcenies in cherry time can dispel. A bird's song contains a clew to its life, and establishes a sympathy, an understanding, between itself and the listener.

I descend a steep hill, and approach the hemlocks through a large sugar-bush. When twenty rods distant, I hear all along the line of the forest the incessant warble of the red-eyed vireo, cheerful and happy as the merry whistle of a schoolboy. He is one of our most common and widely distributed birds. Approach any forest at any hour of the day, in any kind of weather, from May to August, in any of the Middle or Eastern districts, and the chances are that the first note you hear will be his. Rain or shine, before noon or after, in the deep forest or in the village grove, — when it is too hot for the thrushes or too cold and windy for the warblers, — it is never out of time or place for this little minstrel to indulge his cheerful strain. In the deep wilds of the Adirondacks, where few birds are seen and fewer heard, his note was almost constantly in my ear. Always busy, making it a point never to suspend for one moment his occupation to indulge his musical taste, his lay is that of industry and contentment. There is nothing plaintive or especially musical in his performance, but the sentiment expressed is eminently that of cheerfulness. Indeed, the songs of most birds have some human significance, which, I think, is the source of the delight we take in them. The song of the bobolink to me expresses hilarity; the song sparrow's, faith;

the bluebird's, love; the catbird's, pride; the white-eyed flycatcher's, self-consciousness ; that of the hermit thrush, spiritual serenity : while there is something military in the call of the robin.

The red-eye is classed among the flycatchers by some writers, but is much more of a worm-eater, and has few of the traits or habits of the *Muscicapa* or the true *Sylvia*. He resembles somewhat the warbling vireo, and the two birds are often confounded by careless observers. Both warble in the same cheerful strain, but the latter more continuously and rapidly. The red-eye is a larger, slimmer bird, with a faint bluish crown, and a light line over the eye. His movements are peculiar. You may see him hopping among the limbs, exploring the under side of the leaves, peering to the right and left, now flitting a few feet, now hopping as many, and warbling incessantly, occasionally in a subdued tone, which sounds from a very indefinite distance. When he has found a worm to his liking, he turns lengthwise of the limb and bruises its head with his beak before devouring it.

As I enter the woods the slate-colored snowbird · starts up before me and chirps sharply. His protest when thus disturbed is almost metallic in its sharpness. He breeds here, and is not esteemed a snow-bird at all, as he disappears at the near approach of winter, and returns again in spring, like the song sparrow, and is not in any way associated with the cold and the snow. So different are the habits of birds in different localities. Even the crow does not winter here, and is seldom seen after December or before March.

The snowbird, or "black chipping-bird," as it is known among the farmers, is the finest architect of any of the ground-builders known to me. The site of its nest is usually some low bank by the roadside, near a wood. In a slight excavation, with a partially concealed entrance, the exquisite structure is placed. Horse and cow hair are plentifully used, imparting to the interior of the nest great symmetry and firmness as well as softness.

Passing down through the maple arches, barely pausing to observe the antics of a trio of squirrels, — two gray ones and a black one, — I cross an ancient brush fence and am fairly within the old hemlocks, and in one of the most primitive, undisturbed nooks. In the deep moss I tread as with muffled feet, and the pupils of my eyes dilate in the dim, almost religious light. The irreverent red squirrels, however, run and snicker at my approach, or mock the solitude with their ridiculous chattering and frisking.

This nook is the chosen haunt of the winter wren. This is the only place and these the only woods in which I find him in this vicinity. His voice fills these dim aisles, as if aided by some marvelous sounding-board. Indeed, his song is very

strong for so small a bird, and unites in a remarkable degree brilliancy and plaintiveness. I think
of a tremulous vibrating tongue of silver. You
may know it is the song of a wren, from its gushing lyrical character; but you must needs look
sharp to see the little minstrel, especially while in
the act of singing. He is nearly the color of the
ground and the leaves; he never ascends the tall
trees, but keeps low, flitting from stump to stump
and from root to root, dodging in and out of his
hiding-places, and watching all intruders with a
suspicious eye. He has a very pert, almost comical
look. His tail stands more than perpendicular: it
points straight toward his head. He is the least
ostentatious singer I know of. He does not strike
an attitude, and lift up his head in preparation, and,
as it were, clear his throat; but sits there on a log
and pours out his music, looking straight before
him, or even down at the ground. As a songster,
he has but few superiors. I do not hear him after
the first week in July.

While sitting on this soft-cushioned log, tasting
the pungent acidulous wood-sorrel, the blossoms
of which, large and pink-veined, rise everywhere
above the moss, a rufous-colored bird flies quickly
past, and, alighting on a low limb a few rods off,
salutes me with "Whew! Whew!" or "Whoit!
Whoit!" almost as you would whistle for your dog.
I see by his impulsive, graceful movements, and his

dimly speckled breast, that it is a thrush. Presently he utters a few soft, mellow, flute-like notes, one of the most simple expressions of melody to be heard, and scuds away, and I see it is the veery, or Wilson's thrush. He is the least of the thrushes in size, being about that of the common bluebird, and he may be distinguished from his relatives by the dimness of the spots upon his breast. The wood thrush has very clear, distinct oval spots on a white ground ; in the hermit, the spots run more into lines, on a ground of a faint bluish white; in the veery, the marks are almost obsolete, and a few rods off his breast presents only a dull yellowish appearance. To get a good view of him you have only to sit down in his haunts, as in such cases he seems equally anxious to get a good view of you.

From those tall hemlocks proceeds a very fine insect-like warble, and occasionally I see a spray tremble, or catch the flit of a wing. I watch and watch till my head grows dizzy and my neck is in danger of permanent displacement, and still do not get a good view. Presently the bird darts, or, as it seems, falls down a few feet in pursuit of a fly or a moth, and I see the whole of it, but in the dim light am undecided. It is for such emergencies that I have brought my gun. A bird in the hand is worth half a dozen in the bush, even for ornithological purposes; and no sure and rapid progress can be made in the study without taking life,

without procuring specimens. This bird is a warbler, plainly enough, from his habits and manner;
but what kind of warbler? Look on him and name
him: a deep orange or flame-colored throat and
breast; the same color showing also in a line over
the eye and in his crown ; back variegated black
and white. The female is less marked and brilliant. The orange-throated warbler would seem
to be his right name, his characteristic cognomen;
but no, he is doomed to wear the name of some
discoverer, perhaps the first who rifled his nest
or robbed him of his mate,—Blackburn ; hence
Blackburnian warbler. The *burn* seems appropriate enough, for in these dark evergreens his
throat and breast show like flame. He has a very
fine warble, suggesting that of the redstart, but
not especially musical. I find him in no other
woods in this vicinity.

I am attracted by another warble in the same
locality, and experience a like difficulty in getting
a good view of the author of it. It is quite a noticeable strain, sharp and sibilant, and sounds
well amid the old trees. In the upland woods of
beech and maple it is a more familiar sound than
in these solitudes. On taking the bird in hand,
one cannot help exclaiming, "How beautiful!" So
tiny and elegant, the smallest of the warblers ; a
delicate blue back, with a slight bronze-colored
triangular spot between the shoulders ; upper

mandible black ; lower mandible yellow as gold ; throat yellow, becoming a dark bronze, on the breast. Blue yellow-back he is called, though the yellow is much nearer a bronze. He is remarkably delicate and beautiful, — the handsomest as he is the smallest of the warblers known to me. It is never without surprise that I find amid these rugged, savage aspects of nature creatures so fairy and delicate. But such is the law. Go to the sea or climb the mountain, and with the ruggedest and the savagest you will find likewise the fairest and the most delicate. The greatness and the minuteness of nature pass all understanding.

Ever since I entered the woods, even while listening to the lesser songsters, or contemplating the silent forms about me, a strain has reached my ears from out the depths of the forest that to me is the finest sound in nature, — the song of the hermit thrush. I often hear him thus a long way off, sometimes over a quarter of a mile away, when only the stronger and more perfect parts of his music reach me; and through the general chorus of wrens and warblers I detect this sound rising pure and serene, as if a spirit from some remote height were slowly chanting a divine accompaniment. This song appeals to the sentiment of the beautiful in me, and suggests a serene religious beatitude as no other sound in nature does. It is perhaps more of an evening than a morning hymn, though I hear it at all hours of the day. It is very simple, and I can hardly tell the secret of its charm. "O spheral, spheral!" he seems to say; "O holy, holy! O clear away, clear away! O clear up, clear up!" interspersed with the finest trills and the most delicate preludes. It is not a proud, gorgeous strain, like the tanager's or the grosbeak's; suggests no passion or emotion, — nothing personal, — but seems to be the voice of that calm, sweet solemnity one attains to in his best moments. It realizes a peace and a deep, solemn joy that only the finest souls may know. A few nights ago I ascended a mountain to see the world by moonlight, and when near the summit the hermit commenced his evening hymn a few rods from me. Listening to this strain on the lone mountain, with the full moon just rounded from the horizon, the pomp of your cities and the pride of your civilization seemed trivial and cheap.

I have seldom known two of these birds to be singing at the same time in the same locality, rivaling each other, like the wood thrush or the veery. Shooting one from a tree, I have observed another take up the strain from almost the identical perch in less than ten minutes afterward. Later in the day, when I had penetrated the heart of the old Barkpeeling, I came suddenly upon one singing from a low stump, and for a wonder he did not seem alarmed, but lifted up his divine voice as if his

privacy was undisturbed. I open his beak and find
the inside yellow as gold. I was prepared to find it
inlaid with pearls and diamonds, or to see an angel
issue from it.

He is not much in the books. Indeed, I am acquainted with scarcely any writer on ornithology
whose head is not muddled on the subject of our
three prevailing song-thrushes, confounding either
their figures or their songs. A writer in the "Atlantic" [1] gravely tells us the wood thrush is sometimes called the hermit, and then, after describing
the song of the hermit with great beauty and cor-
rectness, coolly ascribes it to the veery! The new
Cyclopædia, fresh from the study of Audubon, says
the hermit's song consists of a single plaintive note,
and that the veery's resembles that of the wood
thrush! The hermit thrush may be easily identified
by his color; his back being a clear olive-brown
becoming rufous on his rump and tail. A quill
from his wing placed beside one from his tail on a
dark ground presents quite a marked contrast.

I walk along the old road, and note the tracks in
the thin layer of mud. When do these creatures
travel here? I have never yet chanced to meet
one. Here a partridge has set its foot ; there, a
woodcock; here, a squirrel or mink; there, a skunk;
there, a fox. What a clear, nervous track reynard
makes! how easy to distinguish it from that of a

[1] For December, 1858.

little dog, — it is so sharply cut and defined! A
dog's track is coarse and clumsy beside it. There
is as much wildness in the track of an animal as
in its voice. Is a deer's track like a sheep's or a
goat's? What winged-footed fleetness and agility
may be inferred from the sharp, braided track of
the gray squirrel upon the new snow! Ah! in nature is the best discipline. How wood-life sharp-
ens the senses, giving a new power to the eye, the
ear, the nose! And are not the rarest and most exquisite songsters wood-birds?

Everywhere in these solitudes I am greeted with
the pensive, almost pathetic note of the wood
pewee. The pewees are the true flycatchers, and
are easily identified. They are very characteristic
birds, have strong family traits and pugnacious
dispositions. They are the least attractive or elegant birds of our fields or forests. Sharp-shouldered,
big-headed, short-legged, of no particular color, of
little elegance in flight or movement, with a disagreeable flirt of the tail, always quarreling with
their neighbors and with one another, no birds are
so little calculated to excite pleasurable emotions in
the beholder, or to become objects of human interest and affection. The kingbird is the best dressed
member of the family, but he is a braggart; and,
though always snubbing his neighbors, is an arrant
coward, and shows the white feather at the slightest display of pluck in his antagonist. I have seen

him turn tail to a swallow, and have known the
little pewee in question to whip him beautifully.
From the great-crested to the little green flycatcher,
their ways and general habits are the same. Slow
in flying from point to point, they yet have a wonderful quickness, and snap up the fleetest insects
with little apparent effort. There is a constant play
of quick, nervous movements underneath their
outer show of calmness and stolidity. They do
not scour the limbs and trees like the warblers,
but, perched upon the middle branches, wait, like
true hunters, for the game to come along. There
is often a very audible snap of the beak as they
seize their prey.

The wood pewee, the prevailing species in this
locality, arrests your attention by his sweet, pathetic
cry. There is room for it also in the deep woods,
as well as for the more prolonged and elevated
strains.

Its relative, the phœbe-bird, builds an exquisite
nest of moss on the side of some shelving cliff or
overhanging rock. The other day, passing by a
ledge near the top of a mountain in a singularly
desolate locality, my eye rested upon one of these
structures, looking precisely as if it grew there, so
in keeping was it with the mossy character of the
rock, and I have had a growing affection for the
bird ever since. The rock seemed to love the nest
and to claim it as its own. I said, what a lesson

in architecture is here! Here is a house that was built, but with such loving care and such beautiful adaptation of the means to the end, that it looks like a product of nature. The same wise economy is noticeable in the nests of all birds. No bird could paint its house white or red, or add aught for show.

At one point in the grayest, most shaggy part of the woods, I come suddenly upon a brood of screech owls, full grown, sitting together upon a dry, moss-draped limb, but a few feet from the ground. I pause within four or five yards of them and am looking about me, when my eye lights upon these gray, motionless figures. They sit perfectly upright, some with their backs and some with their breasts toward me, but every head turned squarely in my direction. Their eyes are closed to a mere black line; through this crack they are watching me, evidently thinking themselves unobserved. The spectacle is weird and grotesque, and suggests something impish and uncanny. It is a new effect, the night side of the woods by daylight. After observing them a moment I take a single step toward them, when, quick as thought, their eyes fly wide open, their attitude is changed, they bend, some this way, some that, and, instinct with life and motion, stare wildly around them. Another step, and they all take flight but one, which stoops low on the branch, and with the look of a frightened cat regards me for a few seconds over its shoulder. They fly swiftly and softly, and disperse through the trees. I shoot one, which is of a tawny red tint, like that figured by Wilson. It is a singular fact that the plumage of these owls presents two totally distinct phases, which "have no relation to sex, age, or season," one being an ashen gray, the other a bright rufous.

Coming to a drier and less mossy place in the woods, I am amused with the golden-crowned thrush, — which, however, is no thrush at all, but a warbler. He walks on the ground ahead of me with such an easy, gliding motion, and with such an unconscious, preoccupied air, jerking his head like a hen or a partridge, now hurrying, now slackening his pace, that I pause to observe him. I sit down, he pauses to observe me, and extends his pretty ramblings on all sides, apparently very much engrossed with his own affairs, but never losing sight of me. But few of the birds are walkers, most being hoppers, like the robin.

Satisfied that I have no hostile intentions, the pretty pedestrian mounts a limb a few feet from the ground, and gives me the benefit of one of his musical performances, a sort of accelerating chant. Commencing in a very low key, which makes him seem at a very uncertain distance, he grows louder and louder till his body quakes and his chant runs into a shriek, ringing in my ear with a peculiar sharpness. This lay may be represented thus: "Teacher, *teacher*, TEACHER, TEACHER, *TEACHER!*" —

the accent on the first syllable and each word uttered with increased force and shrillness. No writer with whom I am acquainted gives him credit for more musical ability than is displayed in this strain. Yet in this the half is not told. He has a far rarer song, which he reserves for some nymph whom he meets in the air. Mounting by easy flights to the top of the tallest tree, he launches into the air with a sort of suspended, hovering flight, like certain of the finches, and bursts into a perfect ecstasy of song, — clear, ringing, copious, rivaling the gold-finch's in vivacity, and the linnet's in melody. This strain is one of the rarest bits of bird melody to be heard, and is oftenest indulged in late in the afternoon or after sundown. Over the woods, hid from view, the ecstatic singer warbles his finest strain. In this song you instantly detect his rela-tionship to the water-wagtail, — erroneously called water-thrush, — whose song is likewise a sudden burst, full and ringing, and with a tone of youthful joyousness in it, as if the bird had just had some unexpected good fortune. For nearly two years this strain of the pretty walker was little more than a disembodied voice to me, and I was puzzled by it as Thoreau by his mysterious night-warbler, which, by the way, I suspect was no new bird at all, but one he was otherwise familiar with. The little bird himself seems disposed to keep the matter a secret, and improves every opportunity to repeat before

you his shrill, accelerating lay, as if this were quite
enough and all he laid claim to. Still, I trust I
am betraying no confidence in making the matter
public here. I think this is preëminently his love-
song, as I hear it oftenest about the mating season.
I have caught half-suppressed bursts of it from two
males chasing each other with fearful speed through
the forest.

Turning to the left from the old road, I wander
over soft logs and gray yielding débris, across the
little trout brook, until I emerge in the overgrown
Barkpeeling, — pausing now and then on the way
to admire a small, solitary white flower which rises
above the moss, with radical, heart-shaped leaves,
and a blossom precisely like the liverwort except
in color, but which is not put down in my botany,
— or to observe the ferns, of which I count six
varieties, some gigantic ones nearly shoulder-high.

At the foot of a rough, scraggy yellow birch, on a
bank of club-moss, so richly inlaid with partridge-
berry and curious shining leaves — with here and
there in the bordering a spire of the false winter-
green strung with faint pink flowers and exhaling
the breath of a May orchard — that it looks too
costly a couch for such an idler, I recline to note
what transpires. The sun is just past the meridian,
and the afternoon chorus is not yet in full tune.
Most birds sing with the greatest spirit and vivacity
in the forenoon, though there are occasional bursts

later in the day in which nearly all voices join ; while it is not till the twilight that the full power and solemnity of the thrush's hymn is felt.

My attention is soon arrested by a pair of hummingbirds, the ruby-throated, disporting themselves in a low bush a few yards from me. The female takes shelter amid the branches, and squeaks exultingly as the male, circling above, dives down as if to dislodge her. Seeing me, he drops like a feather on a slender twig, and in a moment both are gone. Then, as if by a preconcerted signal, the throats are all atune. I lie on my back with eyes half closed, and analyze the chorus of warblers, thrushes, finches, and flycatchers; while, soaring above all, a little withdrawn and alone rises the divine contralto of the hermit. That richly modulated warble proceeding from the top of yonder birch, and which unpracticed ears would mistake for the voice of the scarlet tanager, comes from that rare visitant, the rose-breasted grosbeak. It is a strong, vivacious strain, a bright noonday song, full of health and assurance, indicating fine talents in the performer, but not genius. As I come up under the tree he casts his eye down at me, but continues his song. This bird is said to be quite common in the Northwest, but he is rare in the Eastern districts. His beak is disproportionately large and heavy, like a huge nose, which slightly mars his good looks; but Nature has made it up to him in a blush rose upon his breast, and the most delicate of pink linings to the under side of his wings. His back is variegated black and white, and when flying low the white shows conspicuously. If he passed over your head, you would note the delicate flush under his wings.

That bit of bright scarlet on yonder dead hemlock, glowing like a live coal against the dark background, seeming almost too brilliant for the severe northern climate, is his relative, the scarlet tanager. I occasionally meet him in the deep hemlocks, and know no stronger contrast in nature. I almost fear he will kindle the dry limb on which he alights. He is quite a solitary bird, and in this section seems to prefer the high, remote woods, even going quite to the mountain's top. Indeed, the event of my last visit to the mountain was meeting one of these brilliant creatures near the summit, in full song. The breeze carried the notes far and wide. He seemed to enjoy the elevation, and I imagined his song had more scope and freedom than usual. When he had flown far down the mountain-side, the breeze still brought me his finest notes. In plumage he is the most brilliant bird we have. The bluebird is not entirely blue; nor will the indigo-bird bear a close inspection, nor the goldfinch, nor the summer redbird. But the tanager loses nothing by a near view; the deep scarlet of his body and the black of his wings and tail are quite perfect.

This is his holiday suit; in the fall he becomes a dull yellowish green, — the color of the female the whole season.

One of the leading songsters in this choir of the old Barkpeeling is the purple finch or linnet. He sits somewhat apart, usually on a dead hemlock, and warbles most exquisitely. He is one of our finest songsters, and stands at the head of the finches, as the hermit at the head of the thrushes. His song approaches an ecstasy, and, with the exception of the winter wren's, is the most rapid and copious strain to be heard in these woods. It is quite destitute of the trills and the liquid, silvery, bubbling notes that characterize the wren's; but there runs through it a round, richly modulated whistle, very sweet and very pleasing. The call of the robin is brought in at a certain point with marked effect, and, throughout, the variety is so great and the strain so rapid that the impression is as of two or three birds singing at the same time. He is not common here, and I only find him in these or similar woods. His color is peculiar, and looks as if it might have been imparted by dipping a brown bird in diluted pokeberry juice. Two or three more dippings would have made the purple complete. The female is the color of the song sparrow, a little larger, with heavier beak, and tail much more forked.

In a little opening quite free from brush and

trees, I step down to bathe my hands in the brook, when a small, light slate-colored bird flutters out of the bank, not three feet from my head, as I stoop down, and, as if severely lamed or injured, flutters through the grass and into the nearest bush. As I do not follow, but remain near the nest, she *chips* sharply, which brings the male, and I see it is the speckled Canada warbler. I find no authority in the books for this bird to build upon the ground, yet here is the nest, made chiefly of dry grass, set in a slight excavation in the bank not two feet from the water, and looking a little perilous to anything but ducklings or sandpipers. There are two young birds and one little speckled egg just pipped. But how is this? what mystery is here? One nestling is much larger than the other, monopolizes most of the nest, and lifts its open mouth far above that of its companion, though obviously both are of the same age, not more than a day old. Ah! I see; the old trick of the cow bunting, with a stinging human significance. Taking the interloper by the nape of the neck, I deliberately drop it into the water, but not without a pang, as I see its naked form, convulsed with chills, float downstream. Cruel? So is Nature cruel. I take one life to save two. In less than two days this pot-bellied intruder would have caused the death of the two rightful occupants of the nest; so I step in and turn things into their proper channel again.

It is a singular freak of nature, this instinct which prompts one bird to lay its eggs in the nests of others, and thus shirk the responsibility of rearing its own young. The cow buntings always resort to this cunning trick; and when one reflects upon their numbers, it is evident that these little tragedies are quite frequent. In Europe the parallel case is that of the cuckoo, and occasionally our own cuckoo imposes upon a robin or a thrush in the same manner. The cow bunting seems to have no conscience about the matter, and, so far as I have observed, invariably selects the nest of a bird smaller than itself. Its egg is usually the first to hatch; its young overreaches all the rest when food is brought; it grows with great rapidity, spreads and fills the nest, and the starved and crowded occupants soon perish, when the parent bird removes their dead bodies, giving its whole energy and care to the foster-child.

The warblers and smaller flycatchers are generally the sufferers, though I sometimes see the slate-colored snowbird unconsciously duped in like manner; and the other day, in a tall tree in the woods, I discovered the black-throated green-backed warbler devoting itself to this dusky, overgrown foundling. An old farmer to whom I pointed out the fact was much surprised that such things should happen in his woods without his knowledge.

These birds may be seen prowling through all

parts of the woods at this season, watching for an opportunity to steal their egg into some nest. One day while sitting on a log I saw one moving by short flights through the trees and gradually nearing the ground. Its movements were hurried and stealthy. About fifty yards from me it disappeared behind some low brush, and had evidently alighted upon the ground.

After waiting a few moments I cautiously walked in the direction. When about halfway I accidentally made a slight noise, when the bird flew up, and seeing me, hurried off out of the woods. Arrived at the place, I found a simple nest of dry grass and leaves partially concealed under a prostrate branch. I took it to be the nest of a sparrow. There were three eggs in the nest, and one lying about a foot below it as if it had been rolled out, as of course it had. It suggested the thought that perhaps, when the cowbird finds the full complement of eggs in a nest, it throws out one and deposits its own instead. I revisited the nest a few days afterward and found an egg again cast out, but none had been put in its place. The nest had been abandoned by its owner and the eggs were stale.

In all cases where I have found this egg, I have observed both male and female of the cowbird lingering near, the former uttering his peculiar liquid, glassy note from the tops of the trees.

In July, the young which have been reared in the same neighborhood, and which are now of a dull fawn color, begin to collect in small flocks, which grow to be quite large in autumn.

The speckled Canada is a very superior warbler, having a lively, animated strain, reminding you of certain parts of the canary's, though quite broken and incomplete; the bird, the while, hopping amid the branches with increased liveliness, and indulging in fine sibilant chirps, too happy to keep silent.

His manners are quite marked. He has a habit of courtesying when he discovers you which is very pretty. In form he is an elegant bird, somewhat slender, his back of a bluish lead-color becoming nearly black on his crown : the under part of his body, from his throat down, is of a light, delicate yellow, with a belt of black dots across his breast. He has a fine eye, surrounded by a light yellow ring.

The parent birds are much disturbed by my presence, and keep up a loud emphatic chirping, which attracts the attention of their sympathetic neighbors, and one after another they come to see what has happened. The chestnut-sided and the Blackburnian come in company. The black and yellow warbler pauses a moment and hastens away; the Maryland yellow-throat peeps shyly from the lower bushes and utters his "Fip! fip!" in sympathy; the wood pewee comes straight to the tree overhead, and the red-eyed vireo lingers and lingers, eying me with a curious, innocent look, evidently much puzzled. But all disappear again, one by one, apparently without a word of condolence or encouragement to the distressed pair. I have often noticed among birds this show of sympathy, — if indeed it be sympathy, and not merely curiosity, or desire to be forewarned of the approach of a common danger.

An hour afterward I approach the place, find all still, and the mother bird upon the nest. As I draw near she seems to sit closer, her eyes growing large with an inexpressibly wild, beautiful look. She keeps her place till I am within two paces of her, when she flutters away as at first. In the brief interval the remaining egg has hatched, and the two little nestlings lift their heads without being jostled or overreached by any strange bedfellow. A week afterward and they were flown away, — so brief is the infancy of birds. And the wonder is that they escape, even for this short time, the skunks and minks and muskrats that abound here, and that have a decided partiality for such tidbits.

I pass on through the old Barkpeeling, now threading an obscure cow-path or an overgrown wood-road; now clambering over soft and decayed logs, or forcing my way through a network of briers and hazels; now entering a perfect bower of wild cherry, beech, and soft maple; now emerging into a little grassy lane, golden with buttercups or white with daisies, or wading waist-deep in the red raspberry-bushes.

Whir! whir! whir! and a brood of half-grown partridges start up like an explosion, a few paces from me, and, scattering, disappear in the bushes on all sides. Let me sit down here behind the screen of ferns and briers, and hear this wild hen of the woods call together her brood. At what an early age the partridge flies! Nature seems to concentrate her energies on the wing, making the safety of the bird a point to be looked after first; and while the body is covered with down, and no signs of feathers are visible, the wing-quills sprout and unfold, and in an incredibly short time the young make fair headway in flying.

The same rapid development of wing may be observed in chickens and turkeys, but not in water-fowls, nor in birds that are safely housed in the nest till full-fledged. The other day, by a brook, I came suddenly upon a young sandpiper, a most beautiful creature, enveloped in a soft gray down, swift and nimble and apparently a week or two old, but with no signs of plumage either of body or wing. And it needed none, for it escaped me by taking to the water as readily as if it had flown with wings.

Hark! there arises over there in the brush a soft, persuasive cooing, a sound so subtle and wild and unobtrusive that it requires the most alert and watchful ear to hear it. How gentle and solicitous and full of yearning love! It is the voice of the mother hen. Presently a faint timid "Yeap!" which almost eludes the ear, is heard in various directions, — the young responding. As no danger seems near, the cooing of the parent bird is soon a very audible clucking call, and the young move cautiously in the direction. Let me step never so carefully from my hiding-place, and all sounds instantly cease, and I search in vain for either parent or young.

The partridge is one of our most native and characteristic birds. The woods seem good to be in where I find him. He gives a habitable air to the forest, and one feels as if the rightful occupant was really at home. The woods where I do not find him seem to want something, as if suffering from some neglect of Nature. And then he is such a splendid success, so hardy and vigorous. I think he enjoys the cold and the snow. His wings seem to rustle with more fervency in midwinter. If the snow falls very fast, and promises a heavy storm, he will complacently sit down and allow himself to be snowed under. Approaching him at such times, he suddenly bursts out of the snow at your feet, scattering the flakes in all directions, and goes humming away through the woods like a bomb-shell, — a picture of native spirit and success.

His drum is one of the most welcome and beautiful sounds of spring. Scarcely have the trees expanded their buds, when, in the still April mornings, or toward nightfall, you hear the hum of his devoted wings. He selects not, as you would predict, a dry and resinous log, but a decayed and crumbling one, seeming to give the preference to old oak-logs that are partly blended with the soil. If a log to his taste cannot be found, he sets up his altar on a rock, which becomes resonant beneath his fervent blows. Who has seen the partridge drum? It is the next thing to catching a weasel asleep, though by much caution and tact it may be done. He does not hug the log, but stands very erect, expands his ruff, gives two introductory blows, pauses half a second, and then resumes, striking faster and faster till the sound becomes a continuous, unbroken whir, the whole lasting less than half a minute. The tips of his wings barely brush the log, so that the sound is produced rather by the force of the blows upon the air and upon his own body as in flying. One log will be used for many years, though not by the same drummer. It seems to be a sort of temple and held in great respect. The bird always approaches on foot, and leaves it in the same quiet manner, unless rudely disturbed. He is very cunning, though his wit is not profound. It is difficult to approach him by stealth; you will try many times before succeeding; but seem to pass

by him in a great hurry, making all the noise possible, and with plumage furled he stands as immov-
able as a knot, allowing you a good view, and a
good shot if you are a sportsman.

Passing along one of the old Barkpeelers' roads
which wander aimlessly about, I am attracted by a
singularly brilliant and emphatic warble, proceeding from the low bushes, and quickly suggesting
the voice of the Maryland yellow-throat. Presently
the singer hops up on a dry twig, and gives me a
good view : lead-colored head and neck, becoming
nearly black on the breast; clear olive-green back,
and yellow belly. From his habit of keeping near
the ground, even hopping upon it occasionally, I
know him to be a ground warbler; from his dark
breast the ornithologist has added the expletive
mourning, hence the mourning ground warbler.

Of this bird both Wilson and Audubon confessed
their comparative ignorance, neither ever having
seen its nest or become acquainted with its haunts
and general habits. Its song is quite striking and
novel, though its voice at once suggests the class of
warblers to which it belongs. It is very shy and
wary, flying but a few feet at a time, and studiously
concealing itself from your view. I discover but
one pair here. The female has food in her beak,
but carefully avoids betraying the locality of her
nest. The ground warblers all have one notable
feature, — very beautiful legs, as white and delicate

as if they had always worn silk stockings and satin slippers. High tree warblers have dark brown or black legs and more brilliant plumage, but less musical ability.

The chestnut-sided belongs to the latter class. He is quite common in these woods, as in all the woods about. He is one of the rarest and handsomest of the warblers; his white breast and throat, chestnut sides, and yellow crown show conspicuously. Last year I found the nest of one in an uplying beech wood, in a low bush near the roadside, where cows passed and browsed daily. Things went on smoothly till the cow bunting stole her egg into it, when other mishaps followed, and the nest was soon empty. A characteristic attitude of the male during this season is a slight drooping of the wings, and tail a little elevated, which gives him a very smart, bantam-like appearance. His song is fine and hurried, and not much of itself, but has its place in the general chorus.

A far sweeter strain, falling on the ear with the true sylvan cadence, is that of the black-throated green-backed warbler, whom I meet at various points. He has no superiors among the true *Sylvia*. His song is very plain and simple, but remarkably pure and tender, and might be indicated by straight lines, thus, —— —— √‾; the first two marks representing two sweet, silvery notes, in the same pitch of voice, and quite unaccented; the latter marks, the concluding notes, wherein the tone and inflection are changed. The throat and breast of the male are a rich black like velvet, his face yellow, and his back a yellowish green.

Beyond the Barkpeeling, where the woods are mingled hemlock, beech, and birch, the languid midsummer note of the black-throated blue-back falls on my ear. "Twea, twea, twea-e-e!" in the upward slide, and with the peculiar *z-ing* of summer insects, but not destitute of a certain plaintive cadence. It is one of the most languid, unhurried sounds in all the woods. I feel like reclining upon the dry leaves at once. Audubon says he has never heard his love-song; but this is all the love-song he has, and he is evidently a very plain hero with his little brown mistress. He assumes few attitudes, and is not a bold and striking gymnast, like many of his kindred. He has a preference for dense woods of beech and maple, moves slowly amid the lower branches and smaller growths, keeping from eight to ten feet from the ground, and repeating now and then his listless, indolent strain. His back and crown are dark blue ; his throat and breast, black; his belly, pure white; and he has a white spot on each wing.

Here and there I meet the black and white creeping warbler, whose fine strain reminds me of hairwire. It is unquestionably the finest bird-song to be heard. Few insect strains will compare with it in this respect; while it has none of the harsh, brassy character of the latter, being very delicate and tender.

That sharp, uninterrupted, but still continued warble, which, before one has learned to discriminate closely, he is apt to confound with the red-eyed vireo's, is that of the solitary warbling vireo, — a bird slightly larger, much rarer, and with a louder, less cheerful and happy strain. I see him hopping along lengthwise of the limbs, and note the orange tinge of his breast and sides and the white circle around his eye.

But the declining sun and the deepening shadows admonish me that this ramble must be brought to a close, even though only the leading characters in this chorus of forty songsters have been described, and only a small portion of the venerable old woods explored. In a secluded swampy corner of the old Barkpeeling, where I find the great purple orchis in bloom, and where the foot of man or beast seems never to have trod, I linger long, contemplating the wonderful display of lichens and mosses that overrun both the smaller and the larger growths. Every bush and branch and sprig is dressed up in the most rich and fantastic of liveries; and, crowning all, the long bearded moss festoons the branches or sways gracefully from the limbs. Every twig looks a century old, though green leaves tip the end of it. A young yellow birch has a venerable, patriarchal look, and seems ill at ease under such premature honors. A decayed hemlock is draped as if by hands for some solemn festival.

Mounting toward the upland again, I pause reverently as the hush and stillness of twilight come upon the woods. It is the sweetest, ripest hour of the day. And as the hermit's evening hymn goes up from the deep solitude below me, I experience that serene exaltation of sentiment of which music, literature, and religion are but the faint types and symbols.

1865.

III

THE ADIRONDACKS

WHEN I went to the Adirondacks, which was in the summer of 1863, I was in the first flush of my ornithological studies, and was curious, above all else, to know what birds I should find in these solitudes, — what new ones, and what ones already known to me.

In visiting vast, primitive, far-off woods one naturally expects to find something rare and precious, or something entirely new, but it commonly happens that one is disappointed. Thoreau made three excursions into the Maine woods, and, though he started the moose and caribou, had nothing more novel to report by way of bird notes than the songs of the wood thrush and the pewee. This was about my own experience in the Adirondacks. The birds for the most part prefer the vicinity of settlements and clearings, and it was at such places that I saw the greatest number and variety.

At the clearing of an old hunter and pioneer by the name of Hewett, where we paused a couple of days on first entering the woods, I saw many old friends and made some new acquaintances. The snowbird was very abundant here, as it had been at various points along the route after leaving Lake George. As I went out to the spring in the morning to wash myself, a purple finch flew up before me, having already performed its ablutions. I had first observed this bird the winter before in the Highlands of the Hudson, where, during several clear but cold February mornings, a troop of them sang most charmingly in a tree in front of my house. The meeting with the bird here in its breeding haunts was a pleasant surprise. During the day I observed several pine finches, — a dark brown or brindlish bird, allied to the common yellowbird, which it much resembles in its manner and habits. They lingered familiarly about the house, sometimes alighting in a small tree within a few feet of it. In one of the stumpy fields I saw an old favorite in the grass finch or vesper sparrow. It was sitting on a tall charred stub with food in its beak. But all along the borders of the woods and in the bushy parts of the fields there was a new song that I was puzzled in tracing to the author. It was most noticeable in the morning and at twilight, but was at all times singularly secret and elusive. I at last discovered that it was the white-throated sparrow, a common bird all through this region. Its song is very delicate and plaintive, — a thin, wavering, tremulous whistle, which disappoints one, however, as it ends when it seems only to have begun. If the

A Cabin in the Adirondacks

bird could give us the finishing strain of which this seems only the prelude, it would stand first among feathered songsters.

By a little trout brook in a low part of the woods adjoining the clearing, I had a good time pursuing and identifying a number of warblers, — the speckled Canada, the black-throated blue, the yellow-rumped, and Audubon's warbler. The latter, which was leading its troop of young through a thick undergrowth on the banks of the creek where insects were plenty, was new to me.

It being August, the birds were all moulting, and sang only fitfully and by brief snatches. I remember hearing but one robin during the whole trip. This was by the Boreas River in the deep forest. It was like the voice of an old friend speaking my name.

From Hewett's, after engaging his youngest son, — the "Bub" of the family, — a young man about twenty and a thorough woodsman, as guide, we took to the woods in good earnest, our destination being the Stillwater of the Boreas, — a long, deep, dark reach in one of the remote branches of the Hudson, about six miles distant. Here we paused a couple of days, putting up in a dilapidated lumbermen's shanty, and cooking our fish over an old stove which had been left there. The most noteworthy incident of our stay at this point was the taking by myself of half a dozen splendid trout out of the Stillwater, after the guide had exhausted his art and his patience with very insignificant results. The place had a very trouty look; but as the season was late and the river warm, I knew the fish lay in deep water from which they could not be attracted. In deep water accordingly, and near the head of the hole, I determined to look for them. Securing a chub, I cut it into pieces about an inch long, and with these for bait sank my hook into the head of the Stillwater, and just to one side of the main current. In less than twenty minutes I had landed six noble fellows, three of them over one foot long each. The guide and my incredulous companions, who were watching me from the opposite shore, seeing my luck, whipped out their tackle in great haste and began casting first at a respectable distance from me, then all about me, but without a single catch. My own efforts suddenly became fruitless also, but I had conquered the guide, and thenceforth he treated me with the tone and freedom of a comrade and equal.

One afternoon we visited a cave some two miles down the stream, which had recently been discovered. We squeezed and wriggled through a big crack or cleft in the side of the mountain for about one hundred feet, when we emerged into a large dome-shaped passage, the abode, during certain seasons of the year, of innumerable bats, and at all times of primeval darkness. There were various other crannies and pit-holes opening into it, some of which we explored. The voice of running water was everywhere heard, betraying the proximity of the little stream by whose ceaseless corroding the cave and its entrance had been worn. This streamlet flowed out of the mouth of the cave, and came from a lake on the top of the mountain; this accounted for its warmth to the hand, which surprised us all.

Birds of any kind were rare in these woods. A pigeon hawk came prowling by our camp, and the faint piping call of the nuthatches, leading their young through the high trees, was often heard.

On the third day our guide proposed to conduct us to a lake in the mountains where we could float for deer.

Our journey commenced in a steep and rugged ascent, which brought us, after an hour's heavy climbing, to an elevated region of pine forest, years before ravished by lumbermen, and presenting all manner of obstacles to our awkward and incumbered pedestrianism. The woods were largely pine, though yellow birch, beech, and maple were common. The satisfaction of having a gun, should any game show itself, was the chief compensation to those of us who were thus burdened. A partridge would occasionally whir up before us, or a red squirrel snicker and hasten to his den: else the woods appeared quite tenantless. The most noted object was a mammoth pine, apparently the last of a great race, which presided over a cluster of yellow birches, on the side of the mountain.

About noon we came out upon a long, shallow sheet of water which the guide called Bloody-Moose Pond, from the tradition that a moose had been slaughtered there many years before. Looking out over the silent and lonely scene, his eye was the first to detect an object, apparently feeding upon lily-pads, which our willing fancies readily shaped into a deer. As we were eagerly waiting some movement to confirm this impression, it lifted up its head, and, lo! a great blue heron. Seeing us approach, it spread its long wings and flew solemnly across to a dead tree on the other side of the lake, enhancing rather than relieving the loneliness and desolation that brooded over the scene. As we proceeded, it flew from tree to tree in advance of us, apparently loth to be disturbed in its ancient and solitary domain. In the margin of the pond we found the pitcher-plant growing, and here and there in the sand the closed gentian lifted up its blue head.

In traversing the shores of this wild, desolate lake, I was conscious of a slight thrill of expectation, as if some secret of Nature might here be revealed, or some rare and unheard-of game disturbed. There is ever a lurking suspicion that the beginning of things is in some way associated with water, and one may notice that in his private walks he is led by a curious attraction to fetch all the springs and ponds in his route, as if by them was the place for wonders and miracles to happen. Once, while in advance of my companions, I saw, from a high rock, a commotion in the water near the shore, but on reaching the point found only the marks of a musquash.

Pressing on through the forest, after many adventures with the pine-knots, we reached, about the middle of the afternoon, our destination, Nate's Pond, — a pretty sheet of water, lying like a silver mirror in the lap of the mountain, about a mile long and half a mile wide, surrounded by dark forests of balsam, hemlock, and pine, and, like the one we had just passed, a very picture of unbroken solitude.

It is not in the woods alone to give one this impression of utter loneliness. In the woods are sounds and voices, and a dumb kind of companionship; one is little more than a walking tree himself; but come upon one of these mountain lakes, and the wildness stands revealed and meets you face to face. Water is thus facile and adaptive, that it makes the wild more wild, while it enhances culture and art.

The end of the pond which we approached was quite shoal, the stones rising above the surface as in a summer brook, and everywhere showing marks of the noble game we were in quest of, — foot-

prints, dung, and cropped and uprooted lily-pads.
After resting for a half hour, and replenishing our
game-pouches at the expense of the most respectable
frogs of the locality, we filed on through the soft,
resinous pine-woods, intending to camp near the
other end of the lake, where, the guide assured us,
we should find a hunter's cabin ready built. A half-
hour's march brought us to the locality, and a most
delightful one it was, — so hospitable and inviting
that all the kindly and beneficent influences of the
woods must have abided there. In a slight depres-
sion in the woods, about one hundred yards from
the lake, though hidden from it for a hunter's rea-
sons, surrounded by a heavy growth of birch, hemlock, and pine, with a lining of balsam and fir, the
rude cabin welcomed us. It was of the approved
style, three sides inclosed, with a roof of bark and
a bed of boughs, and a rock in front that afforded
a permanent backlog to all fires. A faint voice of
running water was heard near by, and, following
the sound, a delicious spring rivulet was disclosed,
hidden by the moss and débris as by a new fall of
snow, but here and there rising in little well-like
openings, as if for our special convenience. On
smooth places on the logs I noticed female names
inscribed in a female hand; and the guide told us
of an English lady, an artist, who had traversed
this region with a single guide, making sketches.

Our packs unslung and the kettle over, our first

move was to ascertain in what state of preservation a certain dug-out might be, which, the guide averred, he had left moored in the vicinity the summer before, — for upon this hypothetical dug-out our hopes of venison rested. After a little searching, it was found under the top of a fallen hemlock, but in a sorry condition. A large piece had been split out of one end, and a fearful chink was visible nearly to the water-line. Freed from the treetop, however, and calked with a little moss, it floated with two aboard, which was quite enough for our purpose. A jack and an oar were necessary to complete the arrangement, and before the sun had set our professor of wood-craft had both in readiness. From a young yellow birch an oar took shape with marvelous rapidity, — trimmed and smoothed with a neatness almost fastidious, — no makeshift, but an instrument fitted for the delicate work it was to perform.

A jack was made with equal skill and speed. A stout staff about three feet long was placed upright in the bow of the boat, and held to its place by a horizontal bar, through a hole in which it turned easily: a half wheel eight or ten inches in diameter, cut from a large chip, was placed at the top, around which was bent a new section of birch bark, thus forming a rude semicircular reflector. Three candles placed within the circle completed the jack. With moss and boughs seats were arranged, — one in the bow for the marksman, and one in the stern for the oarsman. A meal of frogs and squirrels was a good preparation, and, when darkness came, all were keenly alive to the opportunity it brought. Though by no means an expert in the use of the gun, — adding the superlative degree of enthusiasm to only the positive degree of skill, — yet it seemed tacitly agreed that I should act as marksman and kill the deer, if such was to be our luck.

After it was thoroughly dark, we went down to make a short trial trip. Everything working to satisfaction, about ten o'clock we pushed out in earnest. For the twentieth time I felt in the pocket that contained the matches, ran over the part I was to perform, and pressed my gun firmly, to be sure there was no mistake. My position was that of kneeling directly under the jack, which I was to light at the word. The night was clear, moonless, and still. Nearing the middle of the lake, a breeze from the west was barely perceptible, and noiselessly we glided before it. The guide handled his oar with great dexterity; without lifting it from the water or breaking the surface, he imparted the steady, uniform motion desired. How silent it was! The ear seemed the only sense, and to hold dominion over lake and forest. Occasionally a lily-pad would brush along the bottom, and stooping low I could hear a faint murmuring of the water under the bow: else all was still. Then, almost as by magic, we were encompassed by a huge black ring. The surface of the lake, when we had reached the centre, was slightly luminous from the starlight, and the dark, even forest-line that surrounded us, doubled by reflection in the water, presented a broad, unbroken belt of utter blackness. The effect was quite startling, like some huge conjurer's trick. It seemed as if we had crossed the boundary-line between the real and the imaginary, and this was indeed the land of shadows and of spectres. What magic oar was that the guide wielded that it could transport me to such a realm! Indeed, had I not committed some fatal mistake and left that trusty servant behind, and had not some wizard of the night stepped into his place? A slight splashing in-shore broke the spell and caused me to turn nervously to the oarsman: "Musquash," said he, and kept straight on.

Nearing the extreme end of the pond, the boat gently headed around, and silently we glided back into the clasp of that strange orbit. Slight sounds were heard as before, but nothing that indicated the presence of the game we were waiting for; and we reached the point of departure as innocent of venison as we had set out.

After an hour's delay, and near midnight, we pushed out again. My vigilance and susceptibility were rather sharpened than dulled by the waiting; and the features of the night had also deepened and intensified. Night was at its meridian. The sky had that soft luminousness which may often be observed near midnight at this season, and the "large few stars" beamed mildly down. We floated out into that spectral shadow-land and moved slowly on as before. The silence was most impressive. Now and then the faint *yeap* of some traveling bird would come from the air overhead, or the wings of a bat *whisp* quickly by, or an owl hoot off in the mountains, giving to the silence and loneliness a tongue. At short intervals some noise in-shore would startle me, and cause me to turn inquiringly to the silent figure in the stern.

The end of the lake was reached, and we turned back. The novelty and the excitement began to flag; tired nature began to assert her claims; the movement was soothing, and the gunner slumbered fitfully at his post. Presently something aroused me. "There's a deer," whispered the guide. The gun heard, and fairly jumped in my hand. Listening, there came the cracking of a limb, followed by a sound as of something walking in shallow water. It proceeded from the other end of the lake, over against our camp. On we sped, noiselessly as ever, but with increased velocity. Presently, with a thrill of new intensity, I saw the boat was gradually heading in that direction. Now, to a sportsman who gets excited over a gray squirrel, and forgets that he has a gun on the sudden appearance of a fox, this was a severe trial. I felt suddenly cramped for room, and trimming the boat was out of the question. It seemed that I must make some noise in spite of myself. "Light the jack," said a soft whisper behind me. I fumbled nervously for a match, and dropped the first one. Another was drawn briskly across my knee and broke. A third lighted, but went out prematurely, in my haste to get it up to the jack. What would I not have given to see those wicks blaze! We were fast nearing the shore, — already the lily-pads began to brush along the bottom. Another attempt, and the light took. The gentle motion fanned the blaze, and in a moment a broad glare of light fell upon the water in front of us, while the boat remained in utter darkness.

By this time I had got beyond the nervous point, and had come round to perfect coolness and composure again, but preternaturally vigilant and keen. I was ready for any disclosures; not a sound was heard. In a few moments the trees alongshore were faintly visible. Every object put on the shape of a gigantic deer. A large rock looked just ready to bound away. The dry limbs of a prostrate tree were surely his antlers.

But what are those two luminous spots? Need the reader be told what they were? In a moment the head of a real deer became outlined; then his neck and foreshoulders; then his whole body. There he stood, up to his knees in the water, gazing

fixedly at us, apparently arrested in the movement
of putting his head down for a lily-pad, and evidently thinking it was some new-fangled moon
sporting about there. "Let him have it," said my
prompter, — and the crash came. There was a
scuffle in the water, and a plunge in the woods.
"He's gone," said I. "Wait a moment," said the
guide, "and I will show you." Rapidly running
the canoe ashore, we sprang out, and, holding the
jack aloft, explored the vicinity by its light. There,
over the logs and brush, I caught the glimmer of
those luminous spots again. But, poor thing! there
was little need of the second shot, which was the
unkindest cut of all, for the deer had already fallen
to the ground, and was fast expiring. The success
was but a very indifferent one, after all, as the victim turned out to be only an old doe, upon whom
maternal cares had evidently worn heavily during
the summer.

This mode of taking deer is very novel and
strange. The animal is evidently fascinated or
bewildered. It does not appear to be frightened,
but as if overwhelmed with amazement, or under
the influence of some spell. It is not sufficiently
master of the situation to be sensible of fear, or
to think of escape by flight; and the experiment, to
be successful, must be tried quickly, before the first
feeling of bewilderment passes.

Witnessing the spectacle from the shore, I can conceive of nothing more sudden or astounding. You see no movement and hear no noise, but the light *grows* upon you, and stares and stares like a huge eye from the infernal regions.

According to the guide, when a deer has been played upon in this manner and escaped, he is not to be fooled a second time. Mounting the shore, he gives a long signal snort, which alarms every animal within hearing, and dashes away.

The sequel to the deer-shooting was a little sharp practice with a revolver upon a rabbit, or properly a hare, which was so taken with the spectacle of the camp-fire, and the sleeping figures lying about, that it ventured quite up in our midst; but while testing the quality of some condensed milk that sat uncovered at the foot of a large tree, poor Lepus had his spine injured by a bullet.

Those who lodge with Nature find early rising quite in order. It is our voluptuous beds, and isolation from the earth and the air, that prevents us from emulating the birds and beasts in this respect. With the citizen in his chamber, it is not morning, but breakfast-time. The camper-out, however, feels morning in the air, he smells it, sees it, hears it, and springs up with the general awakening. None were tardy at the row of white chips arranged on the trunk of a prostrate tree, when breakfast was halloed; for we were all anxious to try the venison. Few of us, however, took a second piece. It was black and strong.

The day was warm and calm, and we loafed at leisure. The woods were Nature's own. It was a luxury to ramble through them, — rank and shaggy and venerable, but with an aspect singularly ripe and mellow. No fire had consumed and no lumberman plundered. Every trunk and limb and leaf lay where it had fallen. At every step the foot sank into the moss, which, like a soft green snow, covered everything, making every stone a cushion and every rock a bed, — a grand old Norse parlor; adorned beyond art and upholstered beyond skill.

Indulging in a brief nap on a rug of club-moss carelessly dropped at the foot of a pine-tree, I woke up to find myself the subject of a discussion of a troop of chickadees. Presently three or four shy wood warblers came to look upon this strange creature that had wandered into their haunts; else I passed quite unnoticed.

By the lake, I met that orchard beauty, the cedar waxwing, spending his vacation in the assumed character of a flycatcher, whose part he performed with great accuracy and deliberation. Only a month before I had seen him regaling himself upon cherries in the garden and orchard; but as the dog-days approached he set out for the streams and lakes, to divert himself with the more exciting pursuits of the chase. From the tops of the dead trees along the border of the lake, he would sally out in all directions, sweeping through long curves, alternately mounting and descending, now reaching up for a fly high in air, now sinking low for one near the surface, and returning to his perch in a few moments for a fresh start.

The pine finch was also here, though, as usual, never appearing at home, but with a waiting, expectant air. Here also I met my beautiful singer, the hermit thrush, but with no song in his throat now. A week or two later and he was on his journey southward. This was the only species of thrush I saw in the Adirondacks. Near Lake Sandford, where were large tracts of raspberry and wild cherry, I saw numbers of them. A boy whom we met, driving home some stray cows, said it was the "partridge-bird," no doubt from the resemblance of its note, when disturbed, to the cluck of the partridge.

Nate's Pond contained perch and sunfish but no trout. Its water was not pure enough for trout. Was there ever any other fish so fastidious as this, requiring such sweet harmony and perfection of the elements for its production and sustenance? On higher ground about a mile distant was a trout pond, the shores of which were steep and rocky.

Our next move was a tramp of about twelve miles

through the wilderness, most of the way in a drenching rain, to a place called the Lower Iron Works, situated on the road leading in to Long Lake, which is about a day's drive farther on. We found a comfortable hotel here, and were glad ‘enough to avail ourselves of the shelter and warmth which it offered. There was a little settlement and some quite good farms. The place commands a fine view to the north of Indian Pass, Mount Marcy, and the adjacent mountains. On the afternoon of our arrival, and also the next morning, the view was completely shut off by the fog. But about the middle of the forenoon the wind changed, the fog lifted, and revealed to us the grandest mountain scenery we had beheld on our journey. There they sat about fifteen miles distant, a group of them, — Mount Marcy, Mount McIntyre, and Mount Golden, the real Adirondack monarchs. It was an impressive sight, rendered doubly so by the sudden manner in which it was revealed to us by that scene-shifter the Wind.

I saw blackbirds at this place, and sparrows, and the solitary sandpiper, and the Canada woodpecker, and a large number of hummingbirds. Indeed, I saw more of the latter here than I ever before saw in any one locality. Their squeaking and whirring were almost incessant.

The Adirondack Iron Works belong to the past. Over thirty years ago a company in Jersey City purchased some sixty thousand acres of land lying along the Adirondack River, and abounding in magnetic iron ore. The land was cleared, roads, dams, and forges constructed, and the work of manufacturing iron begun.

At this point a dam was built across the Hudson, the waters of which flowed back into Lake Sandford, about five miles above. The lake itself being some six miles long, tolerable navigation was thus established for a distance of eleven miles, to the Upper Works, which seem to have been the only works in operation. At the Lower Works, besides the remains of the dam, the only vestige I saw was a long low mound, overgrown with grass and weeds, that suggested a rude earthwork. We were told that it was once a pile of wood containing hundreds of cords, cut in regular lengths and corded up here for use in the furnaces.

At the Upper Works, some twelve miles distant, quite a village had been built, which was now entirely abandoned, with the exception of a single family.

A march to this place was our next undertaking. The road for two or three miles kept up from the river and led us by three or four rough, stumpy farms. It then approached the lake and kept along its shores. It was here a dilapidated corduroy structure that compelled the traveler to keep an eye on his feet. Blue jays, two or three small hawks, a solitary wild pigeon, and ruffed grouse were seen along the route. Now and then the lake gleamed through the trees, or we crossed on a shaky bridge some of its arms or inlets. After a while we began to pass dilapidated houses by the roadside. One little frame house I remembered particularly ; the door was off the hinges and leaned against the jambs, the windows had but a few panes left, which glared vacantly. The yard and little garden spot were overrun with a heavy growth of timothy, and the fences had all long since gone to decay. At the head of the lake a large stone building projected from the steep bank and extended over the road. A little beyond, the valley opened to the east, and looking ahead about one mile we saw smoke going up from a single chimney. Pressing on, just as the sun was setting we entered the deserted village. The barking of the dog brought the whole family into the street, and they stood till we came up. Strangers in that country were a novelty, and we were greeted like familiar acquaintances.

Hunter, the head, proved to be a first-rate type of an Americanized Irishman. His wife was a Scotch woman. They had a family of five or six children, two of them grown-up daughters, — modest, comely young women as you would find anywhere. The elder of the two had spent a winter in New York with her aunt, which perhaps made her a little more self-conscious when in the presence of the strange young men. Hunter was hired by the company at a dollar a day to live here and see that things were not wantonly destroyed, but allowed to go to decay properly and decently. He had a substantial roomy frame house and any amount of grass and woodland. He had good barns and kept considerable stock, and raised various farm products, but only for his own use, as the difficulties of transportation to market some seventy miles distant made it no object. He usually went to Ticonderoga on Lake Champlain once a year for his groceries, etc. His post-office was twelve miles below at the Lower Works, where the mail passed twice a week. There was not a doctor, or lawyer, or preacher within twenty-five miles. In winter, months elapse without their seeing anybody from the outside world. In summer, parties occasionally pass through here on their way to Indian Pass and Mount Marcy. Hundreds of tons of good timothy hay annually rot down upon the cleared land.

After nightfall we went out and walked up and down the grass-grown streets. It was a curious and melancholy spectacle. The remoteness and surrounding wildness rendered the scene doubly impressive. And the next day and the next the place was an object of wonder. There were about thirty buildings in all, most of them small frame houses with a door and two windows opening into a small yard in front and a garden in the rear, such as are

usually occupied by the laborers in a country manufacturing district. There was one large two-story
boarding-house, a schoolhouse with a cupola and
a bell in it, and numerous sheds and forges, and a
saw-mill. In front of the saw-mill, and ready to
be rolled to their place on the carriage, lay a large
pile of pine logs, so decayed that one could run his
walking-stick through them. Near by, a building
filled with charcoal was bursting open and the coal
going to waste on the ground. The smelting works
were also much crumbled by time. The schoolhouse was still used. Every day one of the daughters
assembles her smaller brothers and sisters there
and school keeps. The district library contained
nearly one hundred readable books, which were
well thumbed.

The absence of society had made the family all
good readers. We brought them an illustrated
newspaper which was awaiting them in the post-
office at the Lower Works. It was read and reread
with great eagerness by every member of the household.

The iron ore cropped out on every hand. There
was apparently mountains of it; one could see it in
the stones along the road. But the difficulties met
with in separating the iron from its alloys, together
with the expense of transportation and the failure
of certain railroad schemes, caused the works to be
abandoned. No doubt the time is not distant when

these obstacles will be overcome and this region reopened.

At present it is an admirable place to go to. There is fishing and hunting and boating and mountain-climbing within easy reach, and a good roof over your head at night, which is no small matter. One is often disqualified for enjoying the woods after he gets there by the loss of sleep and of proper food taken at seasonable times. This point attended to, one is in the humor for any enterprise.

About half a mile northeast of the village is Lake Henderson, a very irregular and picturesque sheet of water, surrounded by dark evergreen forests, and abutted by two or three bold promontories with mottled white and gray rocks. Its greatest extent in any one direction is perhaps less than a mile. Its waters are perfectly clear and abound in lake trout. A considerable stream flows into it, which comes down from Indian Pass.

A mile south of the village is Lake Sandford. This is a more open and exposed sheet of water and much larger. From some parts of it Mount Marcy and the gorge of the Indian Pass are seen to excellent advantage. The Indian Pass shows as a huge cleft in the mountain, the gray walls rising on one side perpendicularly for many hundred feet. This lake abounds in white and yellow perch and in pickerel; of the latter single specimens are often caught which weigh fifteen pounds. There were a

few wild ducks on both lakes. A brood of the
goosander or red merganser, the young not yet able
to fly, were the occasion of some spirited rowing.
But with two pairs of oars in a trim light skiff, it
was impossible to come up with them. Yet we
could not resist the temptation to give them a chase
every day when we first came on the lake. It
needed a good long pull to sober us down so we
could fish.

The land on the east side of the lake had been
burnt over, and was now mostly grown up with
wild cherry and red raspberry bushes. Ruffed
grouse were found here in great numbers. The
Canada grouse was also common. I shot eight of
the latter in less than an hour on one occasion; the
eighth one, which was an old male, was killed with
smooth pebble-stones, my shot having run short.
The wounded bird ran under a pile of brush, like
a frightened hen. Thrusting a forked stick down
through the interstices, I soon stopped his breathing.
Wild pigeons were quite numerous also. These
latter recall a singular freak of the sharp-shinned
hawk. A flock of pigeons alighted on the top of a
dead hemlock standing in the edge of a swamp. I
got over the fence and moved toward them across
an open space. I had not taken many steps when,
on looking up, I saw the whole flock again in motion
flying very rapidly around the butt of a hill. Just
then this hawk alighted on the same tree. I stepped

back into the road and paused a moment, in doubt which course to go. At that instant the little hawk launched into the air and came as straight as an arrow toward me. I looked in amazement, but in less than half a minute he was within fifty feet of my face, coming full tilt as if he had sighted my nose. Almost in self-defense I let fly one barrel of my gun, and the mangled form of the audacious marauder fell literally between my feet.

Of wild animals, such as bears, panthers, wolves, wildcats, etc., we neither saw nor heard any in the Adirondacks. "A howling wilderness," Thoreau says, "seldom ever howls. The howling is chiefly done by the imagination of the traveler." Hunter said he often saw bear-tracks in the snow, but had never yet met Bruin. Deer are more or less abundant everywhere, and one old sportsman declares there is yet a single moose in these mountains. On our return, a pioneer settler, at whose house we stayed overnight, told us a long adventure he had had with a panther. He related how it screamed, how it followed him in the brush, how he took to his boat, how its eyes gleamed from the shore, and how he fired his rifle at them with fatal effect. His wife in the mean time took something from a drawer, and, as her husband finished his recital, she produced a toe-nail of the identical animal with marked dramatic effect.

But better than fish or game or grand scenery, or

any adventure by night or day, is the wordless intercourse with rude Nature one has on these expeditions. It is something to press the pulse of our old mother by mountain lakes and streams, and know what health and vigor are in her veins, and how regardless of observation she deports herself.

1866.

IV

BIRDS'-NESTS

HOW alert and vigilant the birds are, even when absorbed in building their nests! In an open space in the woods I see a pair of cedar-birds collecting moss from the top of a dead tree. Following the direction in which they fly, I soon discover the nest placed in the fork of a small soft maple, which stands amid a thick growth of wild cherry-trees and young beeches. Carefully concealing myself beneath it, without any fear that the workmen will hit me with a chip or let fall a tool, I await the return of the busy pair. Presently I hear the well-known note, and the female sweeps down and settles unsuspectingly into the half-finished structure. Hardly have her wings rested before her eye has penetrated my screen, and with a hurried movement of alarm she darts away. In a moment the male, with a tuft of wool in his beak (for there is a sheep pasture near), joins her, and the two reconnoitre the premises from the surrounding bushes. With their beaks still loaded, they move around with a frightened look, and refuse to approach the nest till I have moved off and lain

down behind a log. Then one of them ventures to
alight upon the nest, but, still suspecting all is not
right, quickly darts away again. Then they both
together come, and after much peeping and spying
about, and apparently much anxious consultation,
cautiously proceed to work. In less than half an
hour it would seem that wool enough has been
brought to supply the whole family, real and prospective, with socks, if needles and fingers could be
found fine enough to knit it up. In less than a week
the female has begun to deposit her eggs,— four of
them in as many days, — white tinged with purple,
with black spots on the larger end. After two weeks
of incubation the young are out.

Excepting the American goldfinch, this bird builds
later in the season than any other, — its nest, in our
northern climate, seldom being undertaken till July.
As with the goldfinch, the reason is, probably, that
suitable food for the young cannot be had at an
earlier period.

Like most of our common species, as the robin,
sparrow, bluebird, pewee, wren, etc., this bird
sometimes seeks wild, remote localities in which to
rear its young; at others, takes up its abode near
that of man. I knew a pair of cedar-birds, one season, to build in an apple-tree, the branches of which
rubbed against the house. For a day or two before
the first straw was laid, I noticed the pair carefully exploring every branch of the tree, the female

taking the lead, the male following her with an anxious note and look. It was evident that the wife was to have her choice this time; and, like one who thoroughly knew her mind, she was proceeding to take it. Finally the site was chosen upon a high branch, extending over one low wing of the house. Mutual congratulations and caresses followed, when both birds flew away in quest of building material. That most freely used is a sort of cotton-bearing plant which grows in old wornout fields. The nest is large for the size of the bird, and very soft. It is in every respect a first-class domicile.

On another occasion, while walking or rather sauntering in the woods (for I have discovered that one cannot run and read the book of nature), my attention was arrested by a dull hammering, evidently but a few rods off. I said to myself, "Some one is building a house." From what I had previously seen, I suspected the builder to be a red-headed woodpecker in the top of a dead oak stub near by. Moving cautiously in that direction, I perceived a round hole, about the size of that made by an inch-and-a-half auger, near the top of the decayed trunk, and the white chips of the workman strewing the ground beneath. When but a few paces from the tree, my foot pressed upon a dry twig, which gave forth a very slight snap. Instantly the hammering ceased, and a scarlet head appeared

at the door. Though I remained perfectly motionless, forbearing even to wink till my eyes smarted,
the bird refused to go on with his work, but flew
quietly off to a neighboring tree. What surprised
me was, that, amid his busy occupation down in
the heart of the old tree, he should have been so
alert and watchful as to catch the slightest sound
from without.

The woodpeckers all build in about the same
manner, excavating the trunk or branch of a decayed tree and depositing the eggs on the fine fragments of wood at the bottom of the cavity. Though
the nest is not especially an artistic work, — requiring strength rather than skill, — yet the eggs and
the young of few other birds are so completely
housed from the elements, or protected from their
natural enemies, the jays, crows, hawks, and owls.
A tree with a natural cavity is never selected, but
one which has been dead just long enough to have
become soft and brittle throughout. The bird goes
in horizontally for a few inches, making a hole perfectly round and smooth and adapted to his size,
then turns downward, gradually enlarging the hole,
as he proceeds, to the depth of ten, fifteen, twenty
inches, according to the softness of the tree and the
urgency of the mother bird to deposit her eggs.
While excavating, male and female work alternately.
After one has been engaged fifteen or twenty minutes, drilling and carrying out chips, it ascends to

an upper limb, utters a loud call or two, when its mate soon appears, and, alighting near it on the branch, the pair chatter and caress a moment, then the fresh one enters the cavity and the other flies away.

A few days since I climbed up to the nest of the downy woodpecker, in the decayed top of a sugar maple. For better protection against driving rains, the hole, which was rather more than an inch in diameter, was made immediately beneath a branch which stretched out almost horizontally from the main stem. It appeared merely a deeper shadow upon the dark and mottled surface of the bark with which the branches were covered, and could not be detected by the eye until one was within a few feet of it. The young chirped vociferously as I approached the nest, thinking it was the old one with food; but the clamor suddenly ceased as I put my hand on that part of the trunk in which they were concealed, the unusual jarring and rustling alarming them into silence. The cavity, which was about fifteen inches deep, was gourd-shaped, and was wrought out with great skill and regularity. The walls were quite smooth and clean and new.

I shall never forget the circumstance of observing a pair of yellow-bellied woodpeckers — the most rare and secluded, and, next to the red-headed, the most beautiful species found in our woods — breeding in an old, truncated beech in the Beaverkill

Mountains, an offshoot of the Catskills. We had been traveling, three of us, all day in search of a trout lake, which lay far in among the mountains, had twice lost our course in the trackless forest, and, weary and hungry, had sat down to rest upon a decayed log. The chattering of the young, and the passing to and fro of the parent birds, soon arrested my attention. The entrance to the nest was on the east side of the tree, about twenty-five feet from the ground. At intervals of scarcely a minute, the old birds, one after the other, would alight upon the edge of the hole with a grub or worm in their beaks; then each in turn would make a bow or two, cast an eye quickly around, and by a single movement place itself in the neck of the passage. Here it would pause a moment, as if to determine in which expectant mouth to place the morsel, and then disappear within. In about half a minute, during which time the chattering of the young gradually subsided, the bird would again emerge, but this time bearing in its beak the ordure of one of the helpless family. Flying away very slowly with head lowered and extended, as if anxious to hold the offensive object as far from its plumage as possible, the bird dropped the unsavory morsel in the course of a few yards, and, alighting on a tree, wiped its bill on the bark and moss. This seems to be the order all day,—carrying in and carrying out. I watched the birds for an hour, while my companions were taking their turn in exploring the lay of the land around us, and noted no variation in the programme. It would be curious to know if the young are fed and waited upon in regular order, and how, amid the darkness and the crowded state of the apartment, the matter is so neatly managed. But ornithologists are all silent upon the subject.

This practice of the birds is not so uncommon as it might at first seem. It is indeed almost an invariable rule among all land birds. With woodpeckers and kindred species, and with birds that burrow in the ground, as bank swallows, kingfishers, etc., it is a necessity. The accumulation of the excrement in the nest would prove most fatal to the young.

But even among birds that neither bore nor mine, but which build a shallow nest on the branch of a tree or upon the ground, as the robin, the finches, the buntings, etc., the ordure of the young is removed to a distance by the parent bird. When the robin is seen going away from its brood with a slow, heavy flight, entirely different from its manner a moment before on approaching the nest with a cherry or worm, it is certain to be engaged in this office. One may observe the social sparrow, when feeding its young, pause a moment after the worm has been given and hop around on the brink of the nest observing the movements within.

The instinct of cleanliness no doubt prompts the action in all cases, though the disposition to secrecy or concealment may not be unmixed with it.

The swallows form an exception to the rule, the excrement being voided by the young over the brink of the nest. They form an exception, also, to the rule of secrecy, aiming not so much to conceal the nest as to render it inaccessible.

Other exceptions are the pigeons, hawks, and water-fowls.

But to return. Having a good chance to note the color and markings of the woodpeckers as they passed in and out at the opening of the nest, I saw that Audubon had made a mistake in figuring or describing the female of this species with the red spot upon the head. I have seen a number of pairs of them, and in no instance have I seen the mother bird marked with red.

The male was in full plumage, and I reluctantly shot him for a specimen. Passing by the place again next day, I paused a moment to note how matters stood. I confess it was not without some compunctions that I heard the cries of the young birds, and saw the widowed mother, her cares now doubled, hastening to and fro in the solitary woods. She would occasionally pause expectantly on the trunk of a tree and utter a loud call.

It usually happens, when the male of any species is killed during the breeding season, that the female soon procures another mate. There are, most likely, always a few unmated birds of both sexes within a given range, and through these the broken links may be restored. Audubon or Wilson, I forget which, tells of a pair of fish hawks, or ospreys, that built their nest in an ancient oak. The male was so zealous in the defense of the young that he actually attacked with beak and claw a person who attempted to climb into his nest, putting his face and eyes in great jeopardy. Arming himself with a heavy club, the climber felled the gallant bird to the ground and killed him. In the course of a few days the female had procured another mate. But naturally enough the stepfather showed none of the spirit and pluck in defense of the brood that had been displayed by the original parent. When danger was nigh he was seen afar off, sailing around in placid unconcern.

It is generally known that when either the wild turkey or domestic turkey begins to lay, and afterwards to sit and rear the brood, she secludes herself from the male, who then, very sensibly, herds with others of his sex, and betakes himself to haunts of his own till male and female, old and young, meet again on common ground, late in the fall. But rob the sitting bird of her eggs, or destroy her tender young, and she immediately sets out in quest of a male, who is no laggard when he hears her call. The same is true of ducks and other aquatic fowls.

111

The propagating instinct is strong, and surmounts all ordinary difficulties. No doubt the widowhood I had caused in the case of the woodpeckers was of short duration, and chance brought, or the widow drummed up, some forlorn male, who was not dismayed by the prospect of having a large family of half-grown birds on his hands at the outset.

I have seen a fine cock robin paying assiduous addresses to a female bird as late as the middle of July; and I have no doubt that his intentions were honorable. I watched the pair for half an hour. The hen, I took it, was in the market for the second time that season; but the cock, from his bright, unfaded plumage, looked like a new arrival. The hen resented every advance of the male. In vain he strutted around her and displayed his fine feathers; every now and then she would make at him in a most spiteful manner. He followed her to the ground, poured into her ear a fine, half-suppressed warble, offered her a worm, flew back to the tree again with a great spread of plumage, hopped around her on the branches, chirruped, chattered, flew gallantly at an intruder, and was back in an instant at her side. No use, — she cut him short at every turn.

The *dénouement* I cannot relate, as the artful bird, followed by her ardent suitor, soon flew away beyond my sight. It may not be rash to conclude, however, that she held out no longer than was prudent.

AMERICAN OSPREY OR FISH HAWK

BIRDS'-NESTS

On the whole, there seems to be a system of Women's Rights prevailing among the birds, which, contemplated from the standpoint of the male, is quite admirable. In almost all cases of joint interest, the female bird is the most active. She determines the site of the nest, and is usually the most absorbed in its construction. Generally, she is more vigilant in caring for the young, and manifests the most concern when danger threatens. Hour after hour I have seen the mother of a brood of blue grosbeaks pass from the nearest meadow to the tree that held her nest, with a cricket or grasshopper in her bill, while her better-dressed half was singing serenely on a distant tree or pursuing his pleasure amid the branches.

Yet among the majority of our song-birds the male is most conspicuous both by his color and manners and by his song, and is to that extent a shield to the female. It is thought that the female is humbler clad for her better concealment during incubation. But this is not satisfactory, as in some cases she is relieved from time to time by the male. In the case of the domestic dove, for instance, promptly at midday the cock is found upon the nest. I should say that the dull or neutral tints of the female were a provision of nature for her greater safety at all times, as her life is far more precious to the species than that of the male. The indispensable office of the male reduces itself to little

113

more than a moment of time, while that of his mate extends over days and weeks, if not months.[1]

In migrating northward, the males precede the females by eight or ten days; returning in the fall, the females and young precede the males by about the same time.

After the woodpeckers have abandoned their nests, or rather chambers, which they do after the first season, their cousins, the nuthatches, chickadees, and brown creepers, fall heir to them. These birds, especially the creepers and nuthatches, have many of the habits of the *Picidæ*, but lack their powers of bill, and so are unable to excavate a nest for themselves. Their habitation, therefore, is always second-hand. But each species carries in some soft material of various kinds, or, in other words, furnishes the tenement to its liking. The chickadee arranges in the bottom of the cavity a little

[1] A recent English writer upon this subject presents an array of facts and considerations that do not support this view. He says that, with very few exceptions, it is the rule that, when both sexes are of strikingly gay and conspicuous colors, the nest is such as to conceal the sitting bird ; while, whenever there is a striking contrast of colors, the male being gay and conspicuous, the female dull and obscure, the nest is open and the sitting bird exposed to view. The exceptions to this rule among European birds appear to be very few. Among our own birds, the cuckoos and blue jays build open nests, without presenting any noticeable difference in the coloring of the two sexes. The same is true of the pewees, the kingbird, and the sparrows, while the common bluebird, the oriole, and orchard starling afford examples the other way.

mat of a light felt-like substance, which looks as if it came from the hatter's, but which is probably the work of numerous worms or caterpillars. On this soft lining the female deposits six speckled eggs.

I recently discovered one of these nests in a most interesting situation. The tree containing it, a variety of the wild cherry, stood upon the brink of the bald summit of a high mountain. Gray, time-worn rocks lay piled loosely about, or overtoppled the just visible byways of the red fox. The trees had a half-scared look, and that indescribable wild-ness which lurks about the tops of all remote moun-tains possessed the place. Standing there, I looked down upon the back of the red-tailed hawk as he flew out over the earth beneath me. Following him, my eye also took in farms and settlements and villages and other mountain ranges that grew blue in the distance.

The parent birds attracted my attention by ap-pearing with food in their beaks, and by seeming much put out. Yet so wary were they of revealing the locality of their brood, or even of the precise tree that held them, that I lurked around over an hour without gaining a point on them. Finally a bright and curious boy who accompanied me secreted himself under a low, projecting rock close to the tree in which we supposed the nest to be, while I moved off around the mountain-side. It was not long before the youth had their secret. The tree, which was low and wide-branching, and overrun with lichens, appeared at a cursory glance to contain not one dry or decayed limb. Yet there was one a few feet long, in which, when my eyes were piloted thither, I detected a small round orifice.

As my weight began to shake the branches, the consternation of both old and young was great. The stump of a limb that held the nest was about three inches thick, and at the bottom of the tunnel was excavated quite to the bark. With my thumb I broke in the thin wall, and the young, which were full-fledged, looked out upon the world for the first time. Presently one of them, with a significant chirp, as much as to say, "It is time we were out of this," began to climb up toward the proper entrance. Placing himself in the hole, he looked around without manifesting any surprise at the grand scene that lay spread out before him. He was taking his bearings, and determining how far he could trust the power of his untried wings to take him out of harm's way. After a moment's pause, with a loud chirrup, he launched out and made tolerable headway. The others rapidly followed. Each one, as it started upward, from a sudden impulse, contemptuously saluted the abandoned nest with its excrement.

Though generally regular in their habits and instincts, yet the birds sometimes seem as whimsi-

cal and capricious as superior beings. One is not
safe, for instance, in making any absolute assertion
as to their place or mode of building. Ground-
builders often get up into a bush, and tree-builders
sometimes get upon the ground or into a tussock
of grass. The song sparrow, which is a ground
builder, has been known to build in the knothole
of a fence rail; and a chimney swallow once got
tired of soot and smoke, and fastened its nest on a
rafter in a hay barn. A friend tells me of a pair
of barn swallows which, taking a fanciful turn,
saddled their nest in the loop of a rope that was
pendent from a peg in the peak, and liked it so
well that they repeated the experiment next year.
I have known the social sparrow, or "hairbird," to
build under a shed, in a tuft of hay that hung
down, through the loose flooring, from the mow
above. It usually contents itself with half a dozen
stalks of dry grass and a few long hairs from a cow's
tail loosely arranged on the branch of an apple-tree.
The rough-winged swallow builds in the wall and
in old stone-heaps, and I have seen the robin build
in similar localities. Others have found its nest in
old, abandoned wells. The house wren will build
in anything that has an accessible cavity, from an
old boot to a bombshell. A pair of them once per-
sisted in building their nest in the top of a certain
pump-tree, getting in through the opening above
the handle. The pump being in daily use, the nest

was destroyed more than a score of times. This jealous little wretch has the wise forethought, when the box in which he builds contains two compartments, to fill up one of them, so as to avoid the risk of troublesome neighbors.

The less skillful builders sometimes depart from their usual habit, and take up with the abandoned nest of some other species. The blue jay now and then lays in an old crow's nest or cuckoo's nest. The crow blackbird, seized with a fit of indolence, drops its eggs in the cavity of a decayed branch. I heard of a cuckoo that dispossessed a robin of its nest; of another that set a blue jay adrift. Large, loose structures, like the nests of the osprey and certain of the herons, have been found with half a dozen nests of the blackbirds set in the outer edges, like so many parasites, or, as Audubon says, like the retainers about the rude court of a feudal baron.

The same birds breeding in a southern climate construct far less elaborate nests than when breeding in a northern climate. Certain species of waterfowl, that abandon their eggs to the sand and the sun in the warmer zones, build a nest and sit in the usual way in Labrador. In Georgia, the Baltimore oriole places its nest upon the north side of the tree; in the Middle and Eastern States, it fixes it upon the south or east side, and makes it much thicker and warmer. I have seen one from the

South that had some kind of coarse reed or sedge woven into it, giving it an open-work appearance, like a basket.

Very few species use the same material uniformly. I have seen the nest of the robin quite destitute of mud. In one instance it was composed mainly of long black horse-hairs, arranged in a circular manner, with a lining of fine yellow grass ; the whole presenting quite a novel appearance. In another case the nest was chiefly constructed of a species of rock moss.

The nest for the second brood during the same season is often a mere makeshift. The haste of the female to deposit her eggs as the season advances seems very great, and the structure is apt to be prematurely finished. I was recently reminded of this fact by happening, about the last of July, to meet with several nests of the wood or bush sparrow in a remote blackberry field. The nests with eggs were far less elaborate and compact than the earlier nests, from which the young had flown.

Day after day, as I go to a certain piece of woods, I observe a male indigo-bird sitting on precisely the same part of a high branch, and singing in his most vivacious style. As I approach he ceases to sing, and, flirting his tail right and left with marked emphasis, chirps sharply. In a low bush near by, I come upon the object of his solicitude, — a thick, compact nest composed largely of dry leaves and fine grass, in which a plain brown bird is sitting upon four pale blue eggs.

The wonder is that a bird will leave the apparent security of the treetops to place its nest in the way of the many dangers that walk and crawl upon the ground. There, far up out of reach, sings the bird; here, not three feet from the ground, are its eggs or helpless young. The truth is, birds are the greatest enemies of birds, and it is with reference to this fact that many of the smaller species build.

Perhaps the greatest proportion of birds breed along highways. I have known the ruffed grouse to come out of a dense wood and make its nest at the root of a tree within ten paces of the road, where, no doubt, hawks and crows, as well as skunks and foxes, would be less likely to find it out. Traversing remote mountain-roads through dense woods, I have repeatedly seen the veery, or Wilson's thrush, sitting upon her nest, so near me that I could almost take her from it by stretching out my hand. Birds of prey show none of this confidence in man, and, when locating their nests, avoid rather than seek his haunts.

In a certain locality in the interior of New York, I know, every season, where I am sure to find a nest or two of the slate-colored snowbird. It is under the brink of a low mossy bank, so near the highway that it could be reached from a passing vehicle with a whip. Every horse or wagon or

foot passenger disturbs the sitting bird. She awaits
the near approach of the sound of feet or wheels,
and then darts quickly across the road, barely clearing the ground, and disappears amid the bushes on
the opposite side.

In the trees that line one of the main streets and
fashionable drives leading out of Washington city
and less than half a mile from the boundary, I have
counted the nests of five different species at one
time, and that without any very close scrutiny of
the foliage, while, in many acres of woodland half
a mile off, I searched in vain for a single nest.
Among the five, the nest that interested me most
was that of the blue grosbeak. Here this bird,
which, according to Audubon's observations in Louisiana, is shy and recluse, affecting remote marshes
and the borders of large ponds of stagnant water,
had placed its nest in the lowest twig of the lowest
branch of a large sycamore, immediately over a
great thoroughfare, and so near the ground that a
person standing in a cart or sitting on a horse could
have reached it with his hand. The nest was composed mainly of fragments of newspaper and stalks
of grass, and, though so low, was remarkably well
concealed by one of the peculiar clusters of twigs
and leaves which characterize this tree. The nest
contained young when I discovered it, and, though
the parent birds were much annoyed by my loitering about beneath the tree, they paid little atten-

tion to the stream of vehicles that was constantly passing. It was a wonder to me when the birds could have built it, for they are much shyer when building than at other times. No doubt they worked mostly in the morning, having the early hours all to themselves.

Another pair of blue grosbeaks built in a graveyard within the city limits. The nest was placed in a low bush, and the male continued to sing at intervals till the young were ready to fly. The song of this bird is a rapid, intricate warble, like that of the indigo-bird, though stronger and louder. Indeed, these two birds so much resemble each other in color, form, manner, voice, and general habits that, were it not for the difference in size, — the grosbeak being nearly as large again as the indigo-bird, — it would be a hard matter to tell them apart. The females of both species are clad in the same reddish-brown suits. So are the young the first season.

Of course in the deep, primitive woods, also, are nests; but how rarely we find them! The simple art of the bird consists in choosing common, neutral-tinted material, as moss, dry leaves, twigs, and various odds and ends, and placing the structure on a convenient branch, where it blends in color with its surroundings; but how consummate is this art, and how skillfully is the nest concealed! We occasionally light upon it, but who, unaided by the

movements of the bird, could find it out? During
the present season I went to the woods nearly every
day for a fortnight without making any discoveries
of this kind, till one day, paying them a farewell
visit, I chanced to come upon several nests. A
black and white creeping warbler suddenly became
much alarmed as I approached a crumbling old
stump in a dense part of the forest. He alighted
upon it, chirped sharply, ran up and down its
sides, and finally left it with much reluctance.
The nest, which contained three young birds nearly
fledged, was placed upon the ground, at the foot of
the stump, and in such a position that the color
of the young harmonized perfectly with the bits
of bark, sticks, etc., lying about. My eye rested
upon them for the second time before I made them
out. They hugged the nest very closely, but as I
put down my hand they all scampered off with
loud cries for help, which caused the parent birds
to place themselves almost within my reach. The
nest was merely a little dry grass arranged in a
thick bed of dry leaves.

This was amid a thick undergrowth. Moving on
into a passage of large stately hemlocks, with only
here and there a small beech or maple rising up
into the perennial twilight, I paused to make out
a note which was entirely new to me. It is still
in my ear. Though unmistakably a bird note, it
yet suggested the bleating of a tiny lambkin.

Presently the birds appeared, — a pair of the solitary vireo. They came flitting from point to point, alighting only for a moment at a time, the male silent, but the female uttering this strange, tender note. It was a .rendering into some new sylvan dialect of the human sentiment of maidenly love. It was really pathetic in its sweetness and childlike confidence and joy. I soon discovered that the pair were building a nest upon a low branch a few yards from me. The male flew cautiously to the spot and adjusted something, and the twain moved on, the female calling to her mate at intervals, *love-e, love-e*, with a cadence and tenderness in the tone that rang in the ear long afterward. The nest was suspended to the fork of a small branch, as is usual with the vireos, plentifully lined with lichens, and bound and rebound with masses of coarse spider-webs. There was no attempt at concealment except in the neutral tints, which made it look like a natural growth of the dim, gray woods.

Continuing my random walk, I next paused in a low part of the woods, where the larger trees began to give place to a thick second-growth that covered an old Barkpeeling. I was standing by a large maple, when a small bird darted quickly away from it, as if it might have come out of a hole near its base. As the bird paused a few yards from me, and began to chirp uneasily, my curiosity was at once excited. When I saw it was the female mourn-

ing ground warbler, and remembered that the
nest of this bird had not yet been seen by any
naturalist, — that not even Dr. Brewer had ever
seen the eggs, — I felt that here was something
worth looking for. So I carefully began the search,
exploring inch by inch the ground, the base and
roots of the tree, and the various shrubby growths
about it, till, finding nothing and fearing I might
really put my foot in it, I bethought me to with-
draw to a distance and after some delay return
again, and, thus forewarned, note the exact point
from which the bird flew. This I did, and, returning, had little difficulty in discovering the nest.
It was placed but a few feet from the maple-tree,
in a bunch of ferns, and about six inches from the
ground. It was quite a massive nest, composed
entirely of the stalks and leaves of dry grass, with
an inner lining of fine, dark brown roots. The eggs,
three in number, were of light flesh-color, uniformly specked with fine brown specks. The cavity
of the nest was so deep that the back of the sitting
bird sank below the edge.

In the top of a tall tree, a short distance farther
on, I saw the nest of the red-tailed hawk, — a large
mass of twigs and dry sticks. The young had
flown, but still lingered in the vicinity, and, as I
approached, the mother bird flew about over me,
squealing in a very angry, savage manner. Tufts
of the hair and other indigestible material of the

common meadow mouse lay around on the ground beneath the nest.

As I was about leaving the woods, my hat almost brushed the nest of the red-eyed vireo, which hung basket-like on the end of a low, drooping branch of the beech. I should never have seen it had the bird kept her place. It contained three eggs of the bird's own, and one of the cow bunting. The strange egg was only just perceptibly larger than the others, yet three days after, when I looked into the nest again and found all but one egg hatched, the young interloper was at least four times as large as either of the others, and with such a superabundance of bowels as to almost smother his bedfellows beneath them. That the intruder should fare the same as the rightful occupants, and thrive with them, was more than ordinary potluck; but that it alone should thrive, devouring, as it were, all the rest, is one of those freaks of Nature in which she would seem to discourage the homely virtues of prudence and honesty. Weeds and parasites have the odds greatly against them, yet they wage a very successful war nevertheless.

The woods hold not such another gem as the nest of the hummingbird. The finding of one is an event to date from. It is the next best thing to finding an eagle's nest. I have met with but two, both by chance. One was placed on the horizontal branch of a chestnut-tree, with a solitary green leaf, forming a complete canopy, about an inch and a half above it. The repeated spiteful dartings of the bird past my ears, as I stood under the tree, caused me to suspect that I was intruding upon some one's privacy; and, following it with my eye, I soon saw the nest, which was in process of construction. Adopting my usual tactics of secreting myself near by, I had the satisfaction of seeing the tiny artist at work. It was the female, unassisted by her mate. At intervals of two or three minutes she would appear with a small tuft of some cottony substance in her beak, dart a few times through and around the tree, and alighting quickly in the nest, arrange the material she had brought, using her breast as a model.

The other nest I discovered in a dense forest on the side of a mountain. The sitting bird was disturbed as I passed beneath her. The whirring of her wings arrested my attention, when, after a short pause, I had the good luck to see, through an opening in the leaves, the bird return to her nest, which appeared like a mere wart or excrescence on a small branch. The hummingbird, unlike all others, does not alight upon the nest, but flies into it. She enters it as quick as a flash, but as light as any feather. Two eggs are the complement. They are perfectly white, and so frail that only a woman's fingers may touch them. Incubation lasts about ten days. In a week the young have flown.

The only nest like the hummingbird's, and comparable to it in neatness and symmetry, is that of the blue-gray gnatcatcher. This is often saddled upon the limb in the same manner, though it is generally more or less pendent; it is deep and soft, composed mostly of some vegetable down covered all over with delicate tree-lichens, and, except that it is much larger, appears almost identical with the nest of the hummingbird.

But the nest of nests, the ideal nest, after we have left the deep woods, is unquestionably that of the Baltimore oriole. It is the only perfectly pensile nest we have. The nest of the orchard oriole is indeed mainly so, but this bird generally builds lower and shallower, more after the manner of the vireos.

The Baltimore oriole loves to attach its nest to the swaying branches of the tallest elms, making no attempt at concealment, but satisfied if the position be high and the branch pendent. This nest would seem to cost more time and skill than any other bird structure. A peculiar flax-like substance seems to be always sought after and always found. The nest when completed assumes the form of a large, suspended gourd. The walls are thin but firm, and proof against the most driving rain. The mouth is hemmed or overhanded with horse-hair, and the sides are usually sewed through and through with the same.

Not particular as to the matter of secrecy, the

bird is not particular as to material, so that it be of the nature of strings or threads. A lady friend once told me that, while working by an open window, one of these birds approached during her momentary absence, and, seizing a skein of some kind of thread or yarn, made off with it to its half-finished nest. But the perverse yarn caught fast in the branches, and, in the bird's effort to extricate it, got hopelessly tangled. She tugged away at it all day, but was finally obliged to content herself with a few detached portions. The fluttering strings were an eyesore to her ever after, and, passing and repassing, she would give them a spiteful jerk, as much as to say, "There is that confounded yarn that gave me so much trouble."

From Pennsylvania, Vincent Barnard (to whom I am indebted for other curious facts) sent me this interesting story of an oriole. He says a friend of his curious in such things, on observing the bird beginning to build, hung out near the prospective nest skeins of many-colored zephyr yarn, which the eager artist readily appropriated. He managed it so that the bird used nearly equal quantities of various high, bright colors. The nest was made unusually deep and capacious, and it may be questioned if such a thing of beauty was ever before woven by the cunning of a bird.

Nuttall, by far the most genial of American ornithologists, relates the following: —

"A female (oriole), which I observed attentively, carried off to her nest a piece of lamp-wick ten or twelve feet long. This long string and many other shorter ones were left hanging out for about a week before both the ends were wattled into the sides of the nest. Some other little birds, making use of similar materials, at times twitched these flowing ends, and generally brought out the busy Baltimore from her occupation in great anger.

"I may perhaps claim indulgence for adding a little more of the biography of this particular bird, as a representative also of the instincts of her race. She completed the nest in about a week's time, without any aid from her mate, who indeed appeared but seldom in her company and was now become nearly silent. For fibrous materials she broke, hackled, and gathered the flax of the asclepias and hibiscus stalks, tearing off long strings and flying with them to the scene of her labors. She appeared very eager and hasty in her pursuits, and collected her materials without fear or restraint while three men were working in the neighboring walks and many persons visiting the garden. Her courage and perseverance were indeed truly admirable. If watched too narrowly, she saluted with her usual scolding, *tshrr, tshrr, tshrr*, seeing no reason, probably, why she should be interrupted in her indispensable occupation.

"Though the males were now comparatively silent

on the arrival of their busy mates, I could not help observing this female and a second, continually vociferating, apparently in strife. At last she was observed to attack this *second* female very fiercely, who slyly intruded herself at times into the same tree where she was building. These contests were angry and often repeated. To account for this animosity, I now recollected that *two* fine males had been killed in our vicinity, and I therefore concluded the intruder to be left without a mate; yet she had gained the affections of the consort of the busy female, and thus the cause of their jealous quarrel became apparent. Having obtained the confidence of her faithless paramour, the *second* female began preparing to weave a nest in an adjoining elm by tying together certain pendent twigs as a foundation. The male now associated chiefly with the intruder, whom he even assisted in her labor, yet did not wholly forget his first partner, who called on him one evening in a low, affectionate tone, which was answered in the same strain. While they were thus engaged in friendly whispers, suddenly appeared the rival, and a violent *rencontre* ensued, so that one of the females appeared to be greatly agitated, and fluttered with spreading wings as if considerably hurt. The male, though prudently neutral in the contest, showed his culpable partiality by flying off with his paramour, and for the rest of the evening left the tree to his pugnacious consort. Cares of another kind, more imperious and tender, at length reconciled, or at least terminated, these disputes with the jealous females; and by the aid of the neighboring bachelors, who are never wanting among these and other birds, peace was at length completely restored by the restitution of the quiet and happy condition of monogamy."

Let me not forget to mention the nest under the mountain ledge, the nest of the common pewee, — a modest mossy structure, with four pearl-white eggs, — looking out upon some wild scene and overhung by beetling crags. After all has been said about the elaborate, high-hung structures, few nests perhaps awaken more pleasant emotions in the mind of the beholder than this of the pewee, — the gray, silent rocks, with caverns and dens where the fox and the wolf lurk, and just out of their reach, in a little niche, as if it grew there, the mossy tenement!

Nearly every high projecting rock in my range has one of these nests. Following a trout stream up a wild mountain gorge, not long since, I counted five in the distance of a mile, all within easy reach, but safe from the minks and the skunks, and well housed from the storms. In my native town I know a pine and oak clad hill, round-topped, with a bold, precipitous front extending halfway around it. Near the top, and along this front or side, there crops out a ledge of rocks unusually high and

cavernous. One immense layer projects many feet,
allowing a person or many persons, standing upright,
to move freely beneath it. There is a delicious
spring of water there, and plenty of wild, cool air.
The floor is of loose stone, now trod by sheep and
foxes, once by the Indian and the wolf. How I
have delighted from boyhood to spend a summer
day in this retreat, or take refuge there from a sudden shower! Always the freshness and coolness,
and always the delicate mossy nest of the phœbe-
bird! The bird keeps her place till you are within
a few feet of her, when she flits to a near branch,
and, with many oscillations of her tail, observes you
anxiously. Since the country has become settled,
this pewee has fallen into the strange practice of
occasionally placing its nest under a bridge, hay-
shed, or other artificial structure, where it is subject to all kinds of interruptions and annoyances.
When placed thus, the nest is larger and coarser.
I know a hay-loft beneath which a pair has regularly placed its nest for several successive seasons.
Arranged along on a single pole, which sags down
a few inches from the flooring it was intended to
help support, are three of these structures, marking
the number of years the birds have nested there.
The foundation is of mud with a superstructure of
moss, elaborately lined with hair and feathers.
Nothing can be more perfect and exquisite than the
interior of one of these nests, yet a new one is built

every season. Three broods, however, are frequently reared in it.

The pewees, as a class, are the best architects we have. The kingbird builds a nest altogether admirable, using various soft cotton and woolen substances, and sparing neither time nor material to make it substantial and warm. The green-crested pewee builds its nest in many instances wholly of the blossoms of the white oak. The wood pewee builds a neat, compact, socket-shaped nest of moss and lichens on a horizontal branch. There is never a loose end or shred about it. The sitting bird is largely visible above the rim. She moves her head freely about and seems entirely at her ease, — a circumstance which I have never observed in any other species. The nest of the great-crested flycatcher is seldom free from snake skins, three or four being sometimes woven into it.

About the thinnest, shallowest nest, for its situation, that can be found is that of the turtle-dove. A few sticks and straws are carelessly thrown together, hardly sufficient to prevent the eggs from falling through or rolling off. The nest of the passenger pigeon is equally hasty and insufficient, and the squabs often fall to the ground and perish. The other extreme among our common birds is furnished by the ferruginous thrush, which collects together a mass of material that would fill a half-bushel measure; or by the fish hawk, which adds

to and repairs its nest year after year, till the whole
would make a cart-load.

One of the rarest of nests is that of the eagle, because the eagle is one of the rarest of birds. Indeed,
so seldom is the eagle seen that its presence always
seems accidental. It appears as if merely pausing on the way, while bound for some distant
unknown region. One September, while a youth,
I saw the ring-tailed eagle, the young of the golden
eagle, an immense, dusky bird, the sight of which
filled me with awe. It lingered about the hills
for two days. Some young cattle, a two-year-old
colt, and half a dozen sheep were at pasture on a
high ridge that led up to the mountain, and in
plain view of the house. On the second day this
dusky monarch was seen flying about above them.
Presently he began to hover over them, after the
manner of a hawk watching for mice. He then
with extended legs let himself slowly down upon
them, actually grappling the backs of the young
cattle, and frightening the creatures so that they
rushed about the field in great consternation; and
finally, as he grew bolder and more frequent in his
descents, the whole herd broke over the fence and
came tearing down to the house "like mad." It
did not seem to be an assault with intent to kill, but
was perhaps a stratagem resorted to in order to separate the herd and expose the lambs, which hugged
the cattle very closely. When he occasionally

alighted upon the oaks that stood near, the branch could be seen to sway and bend beneath him. Finally, as a rifleman started out in pursuit of him, he launched into the air, set his wings, and sailed away southward. A few years afterward, in January, another eagle passed through the same locality, alighting in a field near some dead animal, but tarried briefly.

So much by way of identification. The golden eagle is common to the northern parts of both hemispheres, and places its eyrie on high precipitous rocks. A pair built on an inaccessible shelf of rock along the Hudson for eight successive years. A squad of Revolutionary soldiers, also, as related by Audubon, found a nest along this river, and had an adventure with the bird that came near costing one of their number his life. His comrades let him down by a rope to secure the eggs or young, when he was attacked by the female eagle with such fury that he was obliged to defend himself with his knife. In doing so, by a misstroke, he nearly severed the rope that held him, and was drawn up by a single strand from his perilous position.

The bald eagle, also. builds on high rocks, according to Audubon, though Wilson describes the nest of one which he saw near Great Egg Harbor, in the top of a large yellow pine. It was a vast pile of sticks, sods, sedge, grass, reeds, etc., five or six feet high by four broad, and with little or no concavity.

BIRDS'-NESTS

It had been used for many years, and he was told that the eagles made it a sort of home or lodging-place in all seasons.

The eagle in all cases uses one nest, with more or less repair, for several years. Many of our common birds do the same. The birds may be divided, with respect to this and kindred points, into five general classes. First, those that repair or appropriate the last year's nest, as the wren, swallow, bluebird, great-crested flycatcher, owls, eagles, fish hawk, and a few others. Secondly, those that build anew each season, though frequently rearing more than one brood in the same nest. Of these the phœbe-bird is a' well-known example. Thirdly, those that build a new nest for each brood, which includes by far the greatest number of species. Fourthly, a limited number that make no nest of their own, but appropriate the abandoned nests of other birds. Finally, those who use no nest at all, but deposit their eggs in the sand, which is the case with a large number of aquatic fowls.

1866.

V

SPRING AT THE CAPITAL

WITH AN EYE TO THE BIRDS

I CAME to Washington to live in the fall of 1863, and, with the exception of a month each summer spent in the interior of New York, have lived here ever since.

I saw my first novelty in Natural History the day after my arrival. As I was walking near some woods north of the city, a grasshopper of prodigious size flew up from the ground and alighted in a tree. As I pursued him, he proved to be nearly as wild and as fleet of wing as a bird. I thought I had reached the capital of grasshopperdom, and that this was perhaps one of the chiefs or leaders, or perhaps the great High Cock O'lorum himself, taking an airing in the fields. I have never yet been able to settle the question, as every fall I start up a few of these gigantic specimens, which perch on the trees. They are about three inches long, of a gray striped or spotted color, and have quite a reptile look.

The greatest novelty I found, however, was the superb autumn weather, the bright, strong, electric days, lasting well into November, and the general

139

mildness of the entire winter. Though the mercury occasionally sinks to zero, yet the earth is never so seared and blighted by the cold but that in some sheltered nook or corner signs of vegetable life still remain, which on a little encouragement even asserts itself. I have found wild flowers here every month in the year; violets in December, a single houstonia in January (the little lump of earth upon which it stood was frozen hard), and a tiny, weed-like plant, with a flower almost microscopic in its smallness, growing along graveled walks and in old plowed fields in February. The liverwort sometimes comes out as early as the first week in March, and the little frogs begin to pipe doubtfully about the same time. Apricot-trees are usually in bloom on All-Fool's Day and the apple-trees on May Day. By August, mother hen will lead forth her third brood, and I had a March pullet that came off with a family of her own in September. Our calendar is made for this climate. March is a spring month. One is quite sure to see some marked and striking change during the first eight or ten days. This season (1868) is a backward one, and the memorable change did not come till the 10th.

Then the sun rose up from a bed of vapors, and seemed fairly to dissolve with tenderness and warmth. For an hour or two the air was perfectly motionless, and full of low, humming, awakening sounds. The naked trees had a rapt, expectant look. From some unreclaimed common near by came the first strain of the song sparrow; so homely, because so old and familiar, yet so inexpressibly pleasing. Presently a full chorus of voices arose, tender, musical, half suppressed, but full of genuine hilarity and joy. The bluebird warbled, the robin called, the snowbird chattered, the meadowlark uttered her strong but tender note. Over a deserted field a turkey buzzard hovered low, and alighted on a stake in the fence, standing a moment with outstretched, vibrating wings till he was sure of his hold. A soft, warm, brooding day. Roads becoming dry in many places, and looking so good after the mud and the snow. I walk up beyond the boundary and over Meridian Hill. To move along the drying road and feel the delicious warmth is enough. The cattle low long and loud, and look wistfully into the distance. I sympathize with them. Never a spring comes but I have an almost irresistible desire to depart. Some nomadic or migrating instinct or reminiscence stirs within me. I ache to be off.

As I pass along, the high-hole calls in the distance precisely as I have heard him in the North. After a pause he repeats his summons. What can be more welcome to the ear than these early first sounds! They have such a margin of silence!

One need but pass the boundary of Washington

city to be fairly in the country, and ten minutes'
walk in the country brings one to real primitive
woods. The town has not yet overflowed its limits
like the great Northern commercial capitals, and
Nature, wild and unkempt, comes up to its very
threshold, and even in many places crosses it.

The woods, which I soon reach, are stark and
still. The signs of returning life are so faint as to
be almost imperceptible, but there is a fresh, earthy
smell in the air, as if something had stirred here
under the leaves. The crows caw above the wood,
or walk about the brown fields. I look at the gray,
silent trees long and long, but they show no sign.
The catkins of some alders by a little pool have just
swelled perceptibly; and, brushing away the dry
leaves and débris on a sunny slope, I discover the
liverwort just pushing up a fuzzy, tender sprout.
But the waters have brought forth. The little frogs
are musical. From every marsh and pool goes up
their shrill but pleasing chorus. Peering into one
of their haunts, a little body of semi-stagnant water,
I discover masses of frogs' spawn covering the bottom. I take up great chunks of the cold, quivering jelly in my hands. In some places there are
gallons of it. A youth who accompanies me wonders if it would not be good cooked, or if it could
not be used as a substitute for eggs. It is a perfect
jelly, of a slightly milky tinge, thickly imbedded
with black spots about the size of a small bird's

eye. When just deposited it is perfectly transparent. These hatch in eight or ten days, gradually absorb their gelatinous surroundings, and the tiny tadpoles issue forth.

In the city, even before the shop-windows have caught the inspiration, spring is heralded by the silver poplars which line all the streets and avenues. After a few mild, sunshiny March days, you suddenly perceive a change has come over the trees. Their tops have a less naked look. If the weather continues warm, a single day will work wonders. Presently each tree will be one vast plume of gray, downy tassels, while not the least speck of green foliage is visible. The first week in April these long mimic caterpillars lie all about the streets and fill the gutters.

The approach of spring is also indicated by the crows and buzzards, which rapidly multiply in the environs of the city, and grow bold and demonstrative. The crows are abundant here all winter, but are not very noticeable except as they pass high in air to and from their winter quarters in the Virginia woods. Early in the morning, as soon as it is light enough to discern them, there they are, streaming eastward across the sky, now in loose, scattered flocks, now in thick, dense masses, then singly and in pairs or triplets, but all setting in one direction, probably to the waters of eastern Maryland. Toward night they begin to return, flying in the

143

same manner, and directing their course to the wooded heights on the Potomac, west of the city. In spring these diurnal mass movements cease; the clan breaks up, the rookery is abandoned, and the birds scatter broadcast over the land. This seems to be the course everywhere pursued. One would think that, when food was scarcest, the policy of separating into small bands or pairs, and dispersing over a wide country, would prevail, as a few might subsist where a larger number would starve. The truth is, however, that, in winter, food can be had only in certain clearly defined districts and tracts, as along rivers and the shores of bays and lakes.

A few miles north of Newburgh, on the Hudson, the crows go into winter quarters in the same manner, flying south in the morning and returning again at night, sometimes hugging the hills so close during a strong wind as to expose themselves to the clubs and stones of schoolboys ambushed behind trees and fences. The belated ones, that come laboring along just at dusk, are often so overcome by the long journey and the strong current that they seem almost on the point of sinking down whenever the wind or a rise in the ground calls upon them for an extra effort.

The turkey buzzards are noticeable about Washington as soon as the season begins to open, sailing leisurely along two or three hundred feet overhead, or sweeping low over some common or open space where, perchance, a dead puppy or pig or fowl has been thrown. Half a dozen will sometimes alight about some such object out on the commons, and, with their broad dusky wings lifted up to their full extent, threaten and chase each other, while perhaps one or two are feeding. Their wings are very large and flexible, and the slightest motion of them, while the bird stands upon the ground, suffices to lift its feet clear. Their movements when in air are very majestic and beautiful to the eye, being in every respect identical with those of our common hen or red-tailed hawk. They sail along in the same calm, effortless, interminable manner, and sweep around in the same ample spirals. The shape of their wings and tail, indeed their entire effect against the sky, except in size and color, is very nearly the same as that of the hawk mentioned. A dozen at a time may often be seen high in air, amusing themselves by sailing serenely round and round in the same circle.

They are less active and vigilant than the hawk; never poise themselves on the wing, never dive and gambol in the air, and never swoop down upon their prey; unlike the hawks also, they appear to have no enemies. The crow fights the hawk, and the king-bird and crow blackbird fight the crow; but neither takes any notice of the buzzard. He excites the enmity of none, for the reason that he molests none. The crow has an old grudge against the hawk,

145

because the hawk robs the crow's nest and carries
off his young; the kingbird's quarrel with the crow
is upon the same grounds. But the buzzard never
attacks live game, or feeds upon new flesh when old
can be had.

In May, like the crows, they nearly all disappear
very suddenly, probably to their breeding-haunts
near the seashore. Do the males separate from the
females at this time, and go by themselves? At
any rate, in July I discovered that a large number
of buzzards roosted in some woods near Rock Creek,
about a mile from the city limits; and, as they do
not nest anywhere in this vicinity, I thought they
might be males. I happened to be detained late in
the woods, watching the nest of a flying squirrel,
when the buzzards, just after sundown, began to
come by ones and twos and alight in the trees near
me. Presently they came in greater numbers, but
from the same direction, flapping low over the
woods, and taking up their position in the middle
branches. On alighting, each one would blow very
audibly through his nose, just as a cow does when
she lies down; this is the only sound I have ever
heard the buzzard make. They would then stretch
themselves, after the manner of turkeys, and walk
along the limbs. Sometimes a decayed branch
would break under the weight of two or three, when,
with a great flapping, they would take up new po-
sitions. They continued to come till it was quite

dark, and all the trees about me were full. I began
to feel a little nervous, but kept my place. After
it was entirely dark and all was still, I gathered
a large pile of dry leaves and kindled it with a match,
to see what they would think of a fire. Not a sound
was heard till the pile of leaves was in full blaze,
when instantaneously every buzzard started. I
thought the treetops were coming down upon me,
so great was the uproar. But the woods were soon
cleared, and the loathsome pack disappeared in the
night.

About the 1st of June I saw numbers of buzzards sailing around over the great Falls of the
Potomac.

A glimpse of the birds usually found here in the
latter part of winter may be had in the following
extract, which I take from my diary under date of
February 4th: —

"Made a long excursion through the woods and
over the hills. Went directly north from the Capitol for about three miles. The ground bare and
the day cold and sharp. In the suburbs, among
the scattered Irish and negro shanties, came suddenly upon a flock of birds, feeding about like our
northern snow buntings. Every now and then they
uttered a piping, disconsolate note, as if they had a
very sorry time of it. They proved to be shore
larks, the first I had ever seen. They had the walk
characteristic of all larks; were a little larger than

the sparrow; had a black spot on the breast, with much white on the under parts of their bodies. As I approached them the nearer ones paused, and, half squatting, eyed me suspiciously. Presently, at a movement of my arm, away they went, flying exactly like the snow bunting, and showing nearly as much white." (I have since discovered that the shore lark is a regular visitant here in February and March, when large quantities of them are shot or trapped, and exposed for sale in the market. During a heavy snow I have seen numbers of them feeding upon the seeds of various weedy growths in a large market-garden well into town.) "Pressing on, the walk became exhilarating. Followed a little brook, the eastern branch of the Tiber, lined with bushes and a rank growth of green-brier. Sparrows started out here and there, and flew across the little bends and points. Among some pines just beyond the boundary, saw a number of American gold-finches, in their gray winter dress, pecking the pine-cones. A golden-crowned kinglet was there also, a little tuft of gray feathers, hopping about as restless as a spirit. Had the old pine-trees food delicate enough for him also? Farther on, in some low open woods, saw many sparrows,— the fox, white-throated, white-crowned, the Canada, the song, the swamp,— all herding together along the warm and sheltered borders. To my surprise, saw a chewink also, and the yellow-rumped warbler. The purple finch was there likewise, and the Carolina wren and brown creeper. In the higher, colder woods not a bird was to be seen. Returning, near sunset, across the eastern slope of a hill which overlooked the city, was delighted to see a number of grass finches or vesper sparrows, — birds which will be forever associated in my mind with my father's sheep pastures. They ran before me, now flitting a pace or two, now skulking in the low stubble, just as I had observed them when a boy."

A month later, March 4th, is this note: —

"After the second memorable inaguration of President Lincoln, took my first trip of the season. The afternoon was very clear and warm, — real vernal sunshine at last, though the wind roared like a lion over the woods. It seemed novel enough to find within two miles of the White House a simple woodsman chopping away as if no President was being inaugurated! Some puppies, snugly nestled in the cavity of an old hollow tree, he said, belonged to a wild dog. I imagine I saw the 'wild dog,' on the other side of Rock Creek, in a great state of grief and trepidation, running up and down, crying and yelping, and looking wistfully over the swollen flood, which the poor thing had not the courage to brave. This day, for the first time, I heard the song of the Canada sparrow, a soft, sweet note. almost running into a warble. Saw a small, black, velvety butterfly with a yellow border to its wings.

Under a warm bank found two flowers of the houstonia in bloom. Saw frogs' spawn near Piny Branch, and heard the hyla."

Among the first birds that make their appearance in Washington is the crow blackbird. He may come any time after the 1st of March. The birds congregate in large flocks, and frequent groves and parks, alternately swarming in the treetops and filling the air with their sharp jangle, and alighting on the ground in quest of food, their polished coats glistening in the sun from very blackness as they walk about. There is evidently some music in the soul of this bird at this season, though he makes a sad failure in getting it out. His voice always sounds as if he were laboring under a severe attack of influenza, though a large flock of them, heard at a distance on a bright afternoon of early spring, produce an effect not unpleasing. The air is filled with crackling, splintering, spurting, semi-musical sounds, which are like pepper and salt to the ear.

All parks and public grounds about the city are full of blackbirds. They are especially plentiful in the trees about the White House, breeding there and waging war on all other birds. The occupants of one of the offices in the west wing of the Treasury one day had their attention attracted by some object striking violently against one of the window-panes. Looking up, they beheld a crow blackbird pausing in midair, a few feet from the window. On the broad stone window-sill lay the quivering form of a purple finch. The little tragedy was easily read. The blackbird had pursued the finch with such murderous violence that the latter, in its desperate efforts to escape, had sought refuge in the Treasury. The force of the concussion against the heavy plate-glass of the window had killed the poor thing instantly. The pursuer, no doubt astonished at the sudden and novel termination of the career of its victim, hovered a moment, as if to be sure of what had happened, and made off.

(It is not unusual for birds, when thus threatened with destruction by their natural enemy, to become so terrified as to seek safety in the presence of man. I was once startled, while living in a country village, to behold, on entering my room at noon, one October day, a quail sitting upon my bed. The affrighted and bewildered bird instantly started for the open window, into which it had no doubt been driven by a hawk.)

The crow blackbird has all the natural cunning of his prototype, the crow. In one of the inner courts of the Treasury building there is a fountain with several trees growing near. By midsummer the blackbirds become so bold as to venture within this court. Various fragments of food, tossed from the surrounding windows, reward their temerity. When a crust of dry bread defies their beaks, they have been seen to drop it into the water, and, when

151

it has become soaked sufficiently, to take it out again.

They build a nest of coarse sticks and mud, the whole burden of the enterprise seeming to devolve upon the female. For several successive mornings, just after sunrise, I used to notice a pair of them flying to and fro in the air above me as I hoed in the garden, directing their course, on the one hand, to a marshy piece of ground about half a mile distant, and disappearing, on their return, among the trees about the Capitol. Returning, the female always had her beak loaded with building material, while the male, carrying nothing, seemed to act as her escort, flying a little above and in advance of her, and uttering now and then his husky, discordant note. As I tossed a lump of earth up at them, the frightened mother bird dropped her mortar, and the pair scurried away, much put out. Later they avenged themselves by pilfering my cherries.

The most mischievous enemies of the cherries, however, here as at the North, are the cedar waxwings, or "cherry-birds." How quickly they spy out the tree! Long before the cherry begins to turn, they are around, alert and cautious. In small flocks they circle about, high in air, uttering their fine note, or plunge quickly into the tops of remote trees. Day by day they approach nearer and nearer, reconnoitring the premises, and watching the growing fruit. Hardly have the green lobes turned a red cheek to the sun before their beaks have scarred it. At first they approach the tree stealthily, on the side turned from the house, diving quickly into the branches in ones and twos, while the main flock is ambushed in some shade tree not far off. They are most apt to commit their depredations very early in the morning and on cloudy, rainy days. As the cherries grow sweeter the birds grow bolder, till, from throwing tufts of grass, one has to throw stones in good earnest, or lose all his fruit. In June they disappear, following the cherries to the north, where by July they are nesting in the orchards and cedar groves.

Among the permanent summer residents here (one might say city residents, as they seem more abundant in town than out), the yellow warbler or summer yellowbird is conspicuous. He comes about the middle of April, and seems particularly attached to the silver poplars. In every street, and all day long, one may hear his thin, sharp warble. When nesting, the female comes about the yard, pecking at the clothes-line, and gathering up bits of thread to weave into her nest.

Swallows appear in Washington from the first to the middle of April. They come twittering along in the way so familiar to every New England boy. The barn swallow is heard first, followed in a day or two by the squeaking of the cliff swallow. The chimney swallows, or swifts, are not far behind, and remain here, in large numbers, the whole season. The purple martins appear in April, as they pass north, and again in July and August on their return, accompanied by their young.

The national capital is situated in such a vast spread of wild, wooded, or semi-cultivated country, and is in itself so open and spacious, with its parks and large government reservations, that an unusual number of birds find their way into it in the course of the season. Rare warblers, as the black-poll, the yellow red-poll, and the bay-breasted, pausing in May on their northward journey, pursue their insect game in the very heart of the town.

I have heard the veery thrush in the trees near the White House; and one rainy April morning, about six o'clock, he came and blew his soft, mellow flute in a pear-tree in my garden. The tones had all the sweetness and wildness they have when heard in June in our deep northern forests. A day or two afterward, in the same tree, I heard for the first time the song of the ruby-crowned wren, or kinglet, — the same liquid bubble and cadence which characterize the wren-songs generally, but much finer and more delicate than the song of any other variety known to me; beginning in a fine, round, needle-like note, and rising into a full, sustained warble, — a strain, on the whole, remarkably exquisite and pleasing, the singer being all the while as busy as a bee, catching some kind of insects. It is certainly one of our most beautiful bird-songs, and Audubon's enthusiasm concerning its song, as he heard it in the wilds of Labrador, is not a bit extravagant. The song of the kinglet is the only characteristic that allies it to the wrens.

The Capitol grounds, with their fine large trees of many varieties, draw many kinds of birds. In the rear of the building the extensive grounds are peculiarly attractive, being a gentle slope, warm and protected, and quite thickly wooded. Here in early spring I go to hear the robins, catbirds, blackbirds, wrens, etc. In March the white-throated and white-crowned sparrows may be seen, hopping about on the flower-beds or peering slyly from the evergreens. The robin hops about freely upon the grass, notwithstanding the keeper's large-lettered warning, and at intervals, and especially at sunset, carols from the treetops his loud, hearty strain.

The kingbird and orchard starling remain the whole season, and breed in the treetops. The rich, copious song of the starling may be heard there all the forenoon. The song of some birds is like scarlet, — strong, intense, emphatic. This is the character of the orchard starlings, also of the tanagers and the various grosbeaks. On the other hand, the songs of other birds, as of certain of the thrushes, suggest the serene blue of the upper sky.

In February one may hear, in the Smithsonian

grounds, the song of the fox sparrow. It is a strong, richly modulated whistle,— the finest sparrow note I have ever heard.

A curious and charming sound may be heard here in May. You are walking forth in the soft morning air, when suddenly there comes a burst of bobolink melody from some mysterious source. A score of throats pour out one brief, hilarious, tuneful jubilee and are suddenly silent. There is a strange remoteness and fascination about it. Presently you discover its source skyward, and a quick eye will detect the gay band pushing northward. They seem to scent the fragrant meadows afar off, and shout forth snatches of their songs in anticipation.

The bobolink does not breed in the District, but usually pauses in his journey and feeds during the day in the grass-lands north of the city. When the season is backward, they tarry a week or ten days, singing freely and appearing quite at home. In large flocks they search over every inch of ground, and at intervals hover on the wing or alight in the treetops, all pouring forth their gladness at once, and filling the air with a multitudinous musical clamor.

They continue to pass, traveling by night and feeding by day, till after the middle of May, when they cease. In September, with numbers greatly increased, they are on their way back. I am first advised of their return by hearing their calls at night as they fly over the city. On certain nights the sound becomes quite noticeable. I have awakened in the middle of the night, and, through the open window, as I lay in bed, heard their faint notes. The warblers begin to return about the same time, and are clearly distinguished by their timid *yeaps*. On dark, cloudy nights the birds seem confused by the lights of the city, and apparently wander about above it.

In the spring the same curious incident is repeated, though but few voices can be identified. I make out the snowbird, the bobolink, the warblers, and on two nights during the early part of May I heard very clearly the call of the sandpipers.

Instead of the bobolink, one encounters here, in the June meadows, the black-throated bunting, a bird closely related to the sparrows and a very persistent if not a very musical songster. He perches upon the fences and upon the trees by the roadside, and, spreading his tail, gives forth his harsh strain, which may be roughly worded thus: *fscp fscp, fee fee fee.* Like all sounds associated with early summer, it soon has a charm to the ear quite independent of its intrinsic merits.

Outside of the city limits, the great point of interest to the rambler and lover of nature is the Rock Creek region. Rock Creek is a large, rough, rapid stream, which has its source in the interior of Maryland, and flows into the Potomac between Washington and Georgetown. Its course, for five or six miles out of Washington, is marked by great diversity of scenery. Flowing in a deep valley, which now and then becomes a wild gorge with overhanging rocks and high precipitous headlands, for the most part wooded; here reposing in long, dark reaches, there sweeping and hurrying around a sudden bend or over a rocky bed ; receiving at short intervals small runs and spring rivulets, which open up vistas and outlooks to the right and left, of the most charming description,—Rock Creek has an abundance of all the elements that make up not only pleasing but wild and rugged scenery. There is, perhaps, not another city in the Union that has on its very threshold so much natural beauty and grandeur, such as men seek for in remote forests and mountains. A few touches of art would convert this whole region, extending from Georgetown to what is known as Crystal Springs, not more than two miles from the present State Department, into a park unequaled by anything in the world. There are passages between these two points as wild and savage, and apparently as remote from civilization, as anything one meets with in the mountain sources of the Hudson or the Delaware.

One of the tributaries to Rock Creek within this limit is called Piny Branch. It is a small, noisy brook, flowing through a valley of great natural beauty and picturesqueness, shaded nearly all the way by woods of oak, chestnut, and beech, and abounding in dark recesses and hidden retreats.

I must not forget to mention the many springs with which this whole region is supplied, each the centre of some wild nook, perhaps the head of a little valley one or two hundred yards long, through which one catches a glimpse, or hears the voice, of the main creek rushing along below.

My walks tend in this direction more frequently than in any other. Here the boys go, too, troops of them, of a Sunday, to bathe and prowl around, and indulge the semi-barbarous instincts that still lurk within them. Life, in all its forms, is most abundant near water. The rank vegetation nurtures the insects, and the insects draw the birds. The first week in March, on some southern slope where the sunshine lies warm and long, I usually find the hepatica in bloom, though with scarcely an inch of stalk. In the spring runs, the skunk cabbage pushes its pike up through the mould, the flower appearing first, as if Nature had made a mistake.

It is not till about the 1st of April that many wild flowers may be looked for. By this time the hepatica, anemone, saxifrage, arbutus, houstonia, and bloodroot may be counted on. A week later, the claytonia or spring beauty, water-cress, violets, a low buttercup, vetch, corydalis, and potentilla appear. These comprise most of the April flowers, and may be found in great profusion in the Rock Creek and Piny Branch region.

In each little valley or spring run, some one species predominates. I know invariably where to look for the first liverwort, and where the largest and finest may be found. On a dry, gravelly, half-wooded hill-slope the bird's-foot violet grows in great abundance, and is sparse in neighboring districts. This flower, which I never saw in the North, is the most beautiful and showy of all the violets, and calls forth rapturous applause from all persons who visit the woods. It grows in little groups and clusters, and bears a close resemblance to the pansies of the gardens. Its two purple, velvety petals seem to fall over tiny shoulders like a rich cape.

On the same slope, and on no other, I go about the 1st of May for lupine, or sun-dial, which makes the ground look blue from a little distance; on the other or northern side of the slope, the arbutus, during the first half of April, perfumes the wildwood air. A few paces farther on, in the bottom of a little spring run, the mandrake shades the ground with its miniature umbrellas. It begins to push its green finger-points up through the ground by the 1st of April, but is not in bloom till the 1st of May. It has a single white, wax-like flower, with a sweet, sickish odor, growing immediately beneath its broad leafy top. By the same run grow water-

160

Bird's-foot Violets

cresses and two kinds of anemones, — the Pennsylvania and the grove anemone. The bloodroot is very common at the foot of almost every warm slope in the Rock Creek woods, and, where the wind has tucked it up well with the coverlid of dry leaves, makes its appearance almost as soon as the liverwort. It is singular how little warmth is necessary to encourage these earlier flowers to put forth. It would seem as if some influence must come on in advance underground and get things ready, so that, when the outside temperature is propitious, they at once venture out. I have found the bloodroot when it was still freezing two or three nights in the week, and have known at least three varieties of early flowers to be buried in eight inches of snow.

Another abundant flower in the Rock Creek region is the spring beauty. Like most others, it grows in streaks. A few paces from where your attention is monopolized by violets or arbutus, it is arrested by the claytonia, growing in such profusion that it is impossible to set the foot down without crushing the flowers. Only the forenoon walker sees them in all their beauty, as later in the day their eyes are closed, and their pretty heads drooped in slumber. In only one locality do I find the lady's-slipper, — a yellow variety. The flowers that overleap all bounds in this section are the houstonias. By the 1st of April they are very noticeable in warm, damp places along the borders of the woods and in half-cleared fields, but by May these localities are clouded with them. They become visible from the highway across wide fields, and look like little puffs of smoke clinging close to the ground.

On the 1st of May I go to the Rock Creek or Piny Branch region to hear the wood thrush. I always find him by this date leisurely chanting his lofty strain ; other thrushes are seen now also, or even earlier, as Wilson's, the olive-backed, the hermit,— the two latter silent, but the former musical.

Occasionally in the earlier part of May I find the woods literally swarming with warblers, exploring every branch and leaf, from the tallest tulip to the lowest spice-bush, so urgent is the demand for food during their long northern journeys. At night they are up and away. Some varieties, as the blue yellow-back, the chestnut-sided, and the Blackburnian, during their brief stay, sing nearly as freely as in their breeding-haunts. For two or three years I have chanced to meet little companies of the bay-breasted warbler, searching for food in an oak wood on an elevated piece of ground. They kept well up among the branches, were rather slow in their movements, and evidently disposed to tarry but a short time.

The summer residents here, belonging to this class

of birds, are few. I have observed the black and white creeping warbler, the Kentucky warbler, the worm-eating warbler, the redstart, and the gnat-catcher, breeding near Rock Creek.

Of these the Kentucky warbler is by far the most interesting, though quite rare. I meet with him in low, damp places in the woods, usually on the steep sides of some little run. I hear at intervals a clear, strong, bell-like whistle or warble, and presently catch a glimpse of the bird as he jumps up from the ground to take an insect or worm from the under side of a leaf. This is his characteristic movement. He belongs to the class of ground warblers, and his range is very low, indeed lower than that of any other species with which I am acquainted. He is on the ground nearly all the time, moving rapidly along, taking spiders and bugs, overturning leaves, peeping under sticks and into crevices, and every now and then leaping up eight or ten inches to take his game from beneath some overhanging leaf or branch. Thus each species has its range more or less marked. Draw a line three feet from the ground, and you mark the usual limit of the Kentucky warbler's quest for food. Six or eight feet higher bounds the usual range of such birds as the worm-eating warbler, the mourning ground warbler, the Maryland yellow-throat. The lower branches of the higher growths and the higher branches of the lower growths are plainly preferred by the black-throated blue-backed warbler, in those localities where he is found. The thrushes feed mostly on and near the ground, while some of the vireos and the true flycatchers explore the highest branches. But the warblers, as a rule, are all partial to thick, rank undergrowths.

The Kentucky warbler is a large bird for the genus and quite notable in appearance. His back is clear olive-green, his throat and breast bright yellow. A still more prominent feature is a black streak on the side of the face, extending down the neck.

Another familiar bird here, which I never met with in the North, is the gnatcatcher, called by Audubon the blue-gray flycatching warbler. In form and manner it seems almost a duplicate of the catbird on a small scale. It mews like a young kitten, erects its tail, flirts, droops its wings, goes through a variety of motions when disturbed by your presence, and in many ways recalls its dusky prototype. Its color above is a light gray-blue, gradually fading till it becomes white on the breast and belly. It is a very small bird, and has a long, facile, slender tail. Its song is a lisping, chattering, incoherent warble, now faintly reminding one of the goldfinch, now of a miniature catbird, then of a tiny yellow-hammer, having much variety, but no unity and little cadence.

Another bird which has interested me here is the

Louisiana water-thrush, called also large-billed water-thrush, and water-wagtail. It is one of a trio of
birds which has confused the ornithologists much.
The other two species are the well-known golden-
crowned thrush or wood-wagtail, and the northern,
or small, water-thrush.

The present species, though not abundant, is frequently met with along Rock Creek. It is a very
quick, vivacious bird, and belongs to the class of
ecstatic singers. I have seen a pair of these thrushes,
on a bright May day, flying to and fro between
two spring runs, alighting at intermediate points,
the male breaking out into one of the most exuber-
ant, unpremeditated strains I ever heard. Its song
is a sudden burst, beginning with three or four
clear round notes much resembling certain tones of
the clarinet, and terminating in a rapid, intricate
warble.

This bird resembles a thrush only in its color,
which is olive-brown above and grayish white beneath, with speckled throat and breast. Its habits,
manners, and voice suggest those of the lark.

I seldom go the Rock Creek route without being
amused and sometimes annoyed by the yellow-
breasted chat. This bird also has something of the
manners and build of the catbird, yet he is truly an
original. The catbird is mild and feminine compared with this rollicking polyglot. His voice is
very loud and strong and quite uncanny. No sooner

have you penetrated his retreat, which is usually a
thick undergrowth in low, wet localities, near the
woods or in old fields, than he begins his serenade,
which for the variety, grotesqueness, and uncouth-
ness of the notes is not unlike a country *skimmer-
ton*. If one passes directly along, the bird may
scarcely break the silence. But pause a while, or
loiter quietly about, and your presence stimulates
him to do his best. He peeps quizzically at you
from beneath the branches, and gives a sharp feline
mew. In a moment more he says very distinctly,
who, who. Then in rapid succession follow notes
the most discordant that ever broke the sylvan silence. Now he barks like a puppy, then quacks like
a duck, then rattles like a kingfisher, then squalls
like a fox, then caws iike a crow, then mews like a
cat. Now he calls as if to be heard a long way off,
then changes his key, as if addressing the spectator.
Though very shy, and carefully keeping himself
screened when you show any disposition to get a
better view, he will presently, if you remain quiet,
ascend a twig, or hop out on a branch in plain sight,
lop his tail, droop his wings, cock his head, and become very melodramatic. In less than half a minute
he darts into the bushes again, and again tunes up,
no Frenchman rolling his *r*'s so fluently. *C-r-r-r-r-r,
— whrr, — that's it, — chee, — quack, cluck, — yit-
yit-yit, — now hit it, — tr-r-r-r, — when, — caw, caw,
— cut, cut, — tea-boy, — who, who, — mew, mew, —*

and so on till you are tired of listening. Observing one very closely one day, I discovered that he was limited to six notes or changes, which he went through in regular order, scarcely varying a note in a dozen repetitions. Sometimes, when a considerable distance off, he will fly down to have a nearer view of you. And such a curious, expressive flight, — legs extended, head lowered, wings rapidly vibrating, the whole action piquant and droll!

The chat is an elegant bird, both in form and color. Its plumage is remarkably firm and compact. Color above, light olive-green; beneath, bright yellow; beak, black and strong.

The cardinal grosbeak, or Virginia redbird, is quite common in the same localities, though more inclined to seek the woods. It is much sought after by bird-fanciers, and by boy gunners, and consequently is very shy. This bird suggests a British redcoat; his heavy, pointed beak, his high cockade, the black stripe down his face, the expression of weight and massiveness about his head and neck, and his erect attitude, give him a decided, soldier-like appearance; and there is something of the tone of the fife in his song or whistle, while his ordinary note, when disturbed, is like the clink of a sabre. Yesterday, as I sat indolently swinging in the loop of a grapevine, beneath a thick canopy of green branches, in a secluded nook by a spring run, one of these birds came pursuing some kind of insect, but a few feet above me. He hopped about, now and then uttering his sharp note, till, some moth or beetle trying to escape, he broke down through the cover almost where I sat. The effect was like a firebrand coming down through the branches. Instantly catching sight of me, he darted away much alarmed. The female is tinged with brown, and shows but little red except when she takes flight.

By far the most abundant species of woodpecker about Washington is the red-headed. It is more common than the robin. Not in the deep woods, but among the scattered dilapidated oaks and groves, on the hills and in the fields, I hear almost every day his uncanny note, *ktr-rr*, *ktr-r-r*, like that of some larger tree-toad, proceeding from an oak grove just beyond the boundary. He is a strong-scented fellow, and very tough. Yet how beautiful, as he flits about the open woods, connecting the trees by a gentle arc of crimson and white! This is another bird with a military look. His deliberate, dignified ways, and his bright uniform of red, white, and steel-blue, bespeak him an officer of rank.

Another favorite beat of mine is northeast of the city. Looking from the Capitol in this direction, scarcely more than a mile distant, you see a broad green hill-slope, falling very gently, and spreading into a large expanse of meadow-land. The summit, if so gentle a swell of greensward may be said to have a summit, is covered with a grove of large oaks; and, sweeping back out of sight like a mantle, the front line of a thick forest bounds the sides. This emerald landscape is seen from a number of points in the city. Looking along New York Avenue from Northern Liberty Market, the eye glances, as it were, from the red clay of the street, and alights upon this fresh scene in the distance. It is a standing invitation to the citizen to come forth and be refreshed. As I turn from some hot, hard street, how inviting it looks! I bathe my eyes in it as in a fountain. Sometimes troops of cattle are seen grazing upon it. In June the gathering of the hay may be witnessed. When the ground is covered with snow, numerous stacks, or clusters of stacks, are still left for the eye to contemplate.

The woods which clothe the east side of this hill, and sweep away to the east, are among the most charming to be found in the District. The main growth is oak and chestnut, with a thin sprinkling of laurel, azalea, and dogwood. It is the only locality in which I have found the dogtooth violet in bloom, and the best place I know of to gather arbutus. On one slope the ground is covered with moss, through which the arbutus trails its glories.

Emerging from these woods toward the city, one sees the white dome of the Capitol soaring over the green swell of earth immediately in front, and lift-

169

ing its four thousand tons of iron gracefully and lightly into the air. Of all the sights in Washington, that which will survive longest in my memory is the vision of the great dome thus rising cloud-like above the hills.

1868.

VI

BIRCH BROWSINGS

THE region of which I am about to speak lies in the southern part of the State of New York, and comprises parts of three counties, — Ulster, Sullivan, and Delaware. It is drained by tributaries of both the Hudson and Delaware, and, next to the Adirondack section, contains more wild land than any other tract in the State. The mountains which traverse it, and impart to it its severe northern climate, belong properly to the Catskill range. On some maps of the State they are called the Pine Mountains, though with obvious local impropriety, as pine, so far as I have observed, is nowhere found upon them. "Birch Mountains" would be a more characteristic name, as on their summits birch is the prevailing tree. They are the natural home of the black and yellow birch, which grow here to unusual size. On their sides beech and maple abound; while, mantling their lower slopes and darkening the valleys, hemlock formerly enticed the lumberman and tanner. Except in remote or inaccessible localities, the latter tree is now almost never found. In Shandaken and along the Esopus it is about the only product the country yielded, or is likely to yield. Tanneries by the score have arisen and flourished upon the bark, and some of them still remain. Passing through that region the present season, I saw that the few patches of hemlock that still lingered high up on the sides of the mountains were being felled and peeled, the fresh white boles of the trees, just stripped of their bark, being visible a long distance.

Among these mountains there are no sharp peaks, or abrupt declivities, as in a volcanic region, but long, uniform ranges, heavily timbered to their summits, and delighting the eye with vast, undulating horizon lines. Looking south from the heights about the head of the Delaware, one sees, twenty miles away, a continual succession of blue ranges, one behind the other. If a few large trees are missing on the sky line, one can see the break a long distance off.

Approaching this region from the Hudson River side, you cross a rough, rolling stretch of country, skirting the base of the Catskills, which from a point near Saugerties sweep inland; after a drive of a few hours you are within the shadow of a high, bold mountain, which forms a sort of butt-end to this part of the range, and which is simply called High Point. To the east and southeast it slopes down rapidly to the plain, and looks defiance toward the Hudson, twenty miles distant; in the rear of

it, and radiating from it west and northwest, are
numerous smaller ranges, backing up, as it were,
this haughty chief.

From this point through to Pennsylvania, a distance of nearly one hundred miles, stretches the
tract of which I speak. It is a belt of country from
twenty to thirty miles wide, bleak and wild, and
but sparsely settled. The traveler on the New
York and Erie Railroad gets a glimpse of it.

Many cold, rapid trout streams, which flow to
all points of the compass, have their source in the
small lakes and copious mountain springs of this
region. The names of some of them are Mill Brook,
Dry Brook, Willewemack, Beaver Kill, Elk Bush
Kill, Panther Kill, Neversink, Big Ingin, and
Callikoon. Beaver Kill is the main outlet on the
west. It joins the Delaware in the wilds of Han-
cock. The Neversink lays open the region to the
south, and also joins the Delaware. To the east,
various Kills unite with the Big Ingin to form the
Esopus, which flows into the Hudson. Dry Brook
and Mill Brook, both famous trout streams, from
twelve to fifteen miles long, find their way into the
Delaware.

The east or Pepacton branch of the Delaware
itself takes its rise near here in a deep pass between
the mountains. I have many times drunk at a
copious spring by the roadside, where the infant
river first sees the light. A few yards beyond, the

water flows the other way, directing its course
through the Bear Kill and Schoharie Kill into the
Mohawk.

Such game and wild animals as still linger in the
State are found in this region. Bears occasionally
make havoc among the sheep. The clearings at the
head of a valley are oftenest the scene of their
depredations.

Wild pigeons, in immense numbers, used to breed
regularly in the valley of the Big Ingin and about
the head of the Neversink. The treetops for miles
were full of their nests, while the going and coming
of the old birds kept up a constant din. But the
gunners soon got wind of it, and from far and near
were wont to pour in during the spring, and to
slaughter both old and young. This practice soon
had the effect of driving the pigeons all away, and
now only a few pairs breed in these woods.

Deer are still met with, though they are becoming scarcer every year. Last winter near seventy
head were killed on the Beaver Kill alone. I heard
of one wretch, who, finding the deer snowbound,
walked up to them on his snowshoes, and one morning before breakfast slaughtered six, leaving their
carcasses where they fell. There are traditions of
persons having been smitten blind or senseless when
about to commit some heinous offense, but the fact
that this villain escaped without some such visita-
tion throws discredit on all such stories.

The great attraction, however, of this region, is the brook trout, with which the streams and lakes abound. The water is of excessive coldness, the thermometer indicating 44° and 45° in the springs, and 47° or 48° in the smaller streams. The trout are generally small, but in the more remote branches their number is very great. In such localities the fish are quite black, but in the lakes they are of a lustre and brilliancy impossible to describe.

These waters have been much visited of late years by fishing parties, and the name of Beaver Kill is now a potent word among New York sportsmen.

One lake, in the wilds of Callikoon, abounds in a peculiar species of white sucker, which is of excellent quality. It is taken only in spring, during the spawning season, at the time "when the leaves are as big as a chipmunk's ears." The fish run up the small streams and inlets, beginning at nightfall, and continuing till the channel is literally packed with them, and every inch of space is occupied. The fishermen pounce upon them at such times, and scoop them up by the bushel, usually wading right into the living mass and landing the fish with their hands. A small party will often secure in this manner a wagon-load of fish. Certain conditions of the weather, as a warm south or southwest wind, are considered most favorable for the fish to run.

Though familiar all my life with the outskirts of this region, I have only twice dipped into its wilder

175

portions. Once in 1860 a friend and myself traced the Beaver Kill to its source, and encamped by Balsam Lake. A cold and protracted rainstorm coming on, we were obliged to leave the woods before we were ready. Neither of us will soon forget that tramp by an unknown route over the mountains, encumbered as we were with a hundred and one superfluities which we had foolishly brought along to solace ourselves with in the woods; nor that halt on the summit, where we cooked and ate our fish in a drizzling rain; nor, again, that rude log house, with its sweet hospitality, which we reached just at nightfall on Mill Brook.

In 1868 a party of three of us set out for a brief trouting excursion to a body of water called Thomas's Lake, situated in the same chain of mountains. On this excursion, more particularly than on any other I have ever undertaken, I was taught how poor an Indian I should make, and what a ridiculous figure a party of men may cut in the woods when the way is uncertain and the mountains high.

We left our team at a farmhouse near the head of the Mill Brook, one June afternoon, and with knapsacks on our shoulders struck into the woods at the base of the mountain, hoping to cross the range that intervened between us and the lake by sunset. We engaged a good-natured but rather indolent young man, who happened to be stopping at the house, and who had carried a knapsack in the Union armies, to pilot us a couple of miles into the woods so as to guard against any mistakes at the outset. It seemed the easiest thing in the world to find the lake. The lay of the land was so simple, according to accounts, that I felt sure I could go to it in the dark. "Go up this little brook to its source on the side of the mountain," they said. "The valley that contains the lake heads directly on the other side." What could be easier! But on a little further inquiry, they said we should "bear well to the left" when we reached the top of the mountain. This opened the doors again; "bearing well to the left" was an uncertain performance in strange woods. We might bear so well to the left that it would bring us ill. But why bear to the left at all, if the lake was directly opposite? Well, not quite opposite; a little to the left. There were two or three other valleys that headed in near there. We could easily find the right one. But to make assurance doubly sure, we engaged a guide, as stated, to give us a good start, and go with us beyond the bearing-to-the-left point. He had been to the lake the winter before and knew the way. Our course, the first half hour, was along an obscure wood-road which had been used for drawing ash logs off the mountain in winter. There was some hemlock, but more maple and birch. The woods were dense and free from underbrush, the ascent gradual. Most of the way we kept the voice of the

creek in our ear on the right. I approached it once,
and found it swarming with trout. The water was
as cold as one ever need wish. After a while the
ascent grew steeper, the creek became a mere rill
that issued from beneath loose, moss-covered rocks
and stones, and with much labor and puffing we
drew ourselves up the rugged declivity. Every
mountain has its steepest point, which is usually
near the summit, in keeping, I suppose, with the
providence that makes the darkest hour just before
day. It is steep, steeper, steepest, till you emerge
on the smooth level or gently rounded space at
the top, which the old ice-gods polished off so long
ago.

We found this mountain had a hollow in its back
where the ground was soft and swampy. Some
gigantic ferns, which we passed through, came
nearly to our shoulders. We passed also several
patches of swamp honeysuckles, red with blossoms.

Our guide at length paused on a big rock where
the land began to dip down the other way, and concluded that he had gone far enough, and that we
would now have no difficulty in finding the lake.
"It must lie right down there," he said, pointing
with his hand. But it was plain that he was not
quite sure in his own mind. He had several times
wavered in his course, and had shown considerable
embarrassment when bearing to the left across the
summit. Still we thought little of it. We were full

of confidence, and, bidding him adieu, plunged down the mountain-side, following a spring run that we had no doubt led to the lake.

In these woods, which had a southeastern exposure, I first began to notice the wood thrush. In coming up the other side I had not seen a feather of any kind, or heard a note. Now the golden *trillide-de* of the wood thrush sounded through the silent woods. While looking for a fish-pole about halfway down the mountain, I saw a thrush's nest in a little sapling about ten feet from the ground.

After continuing our descent till our only guide, the spring run, became quite a trout brook, and its tiny murmur a loud brawl, we began to peer anxiously through the trees for a glimpse of the lake, or for some conformation of the land that would indicate its proximity. An object which we vaguely discerned in looking under the near trees and over the more distant ones proved, on further inspection, to be a patch of plowed ground. Presently we made out a burnt fallow near it. This was a wet blanket to our enthusiasm. No lake, no sport, no trout for supper that night. The rather indolent young man had either played us a trick, or, as seemed more likely, had missed the way. We were particularly anxious to be at the lake between sundown and dark, as at that time the trout jump most freely.

Pushing on, we soon emerged into a stumpy field, at the head of a steep valley, which swept around toward the west. About two hundred rods below us was a rude log house, with smoke issuing from the chimney. A boy came out and moved toward the spring with a pail in his hand. We shouted to him, when he turned and ran back into the house without pausing to reply. In a moment the whole family hastily rushed into the yard, and turned their faces toward us. If we had come down their chimney, they could not have seemed more astonished. Not making out what they said, I went down to the house, and learned to my chagrin that we were still on the Mill Brook side, having crossed only a spur of the mountain. We had not borne sufficiently to the left, so that the main range, which, at the point of crossing, suddenly breaks off to the southeast, still intervened between us and the lake. We were about five miles, as the water runs, from the point of starting, and over two from the lake. We must go directly back to the top of the range where the guide had left us, and then, by keeping well to the left, we would soon come to a line of marked trees, which would lead us to the lake. So, turning upon our trail, we doggedly began the work of undoing what we had just done, — in all cases a disagreeable task, in this case a very laborious one also. It was after sunset when we turned back, and before we had got halfway up the mountain, it began to be quite dark. We were often obliged to rest our packs against trees and take

breath, which made our progress slow. Finally a
halt was called, beside an immense flat rock which
had paused on its slide down the mountain, and we
prepared to encamp for the night. A fire was built,
the rock cleared off, a small ration of bread served
out, our accoutrements hung up out of the way of
the hedgehogs that were supposed to infest the
locality, and then we disposed ourselves for sleep.
If the owls or porcupines (and I think I heard one
of the latter in the middle of the night) reconnoitred
our camp, they saw a buffalo robe spread upon a
rock, with three old felt hats arranged on one side,
and three pairs of sorry-looking cowhide boots pro-
truding from the other.

When we lay down, there was apparently not a
mosquito in the woods; but the "no-see-ems," as
Thoreau's Indian aptly named the midges, soon
found us out, and after the fire had gone down,
annoyed us much. My hands and wrists suddenly
began to smart and itch in a most unaccountable
manner. My first thought was that they had been
poisoned in some way. Then the smarting extended
to my neck and face, even to my scalp, when I
began to suspect what was the matter. So, wrap-
ping myself up more thoroughly, and stowing my
hands away as best I could, I tried to sleep, being
some time behind my companions, who appeared
not to mind the "no-see-ems." I was further annoyed by some little irregularity on my side of the

couch. The chambermaid had not beaten it up well. One huge lump refused to be mollified, and each attempt to adapt it to some natural hollow in my own body brought only a moment's relief. But at last I got the better of this also and slept. Late in the night I woke up, just in time to hear a golden-crowned thrush sing in a tree near by. It sang as loud and cheerily as at midday, and I thought myself, after all, quite in luck. Birds occasionally sing at night, just as the cock crows. I have heard the hairbird, and the note of the kingbird ; and the ruffed grouse frequently drums at night.

At the first faint signs of day a wood thrush sang, a few rods below us. Then after a little delay, as the gray light began to grow around, thrushes broke out in full song in all parts of the woods. I thought I had never before heard them sing so sweetly. Such a leisurely, golden chant! — it consoled us for all we had undergone. It was the first thing in order, — the worms were safe till after this morning chorus. I judged that the birds roosted but a few feet from the ground. In fact, a bird in all cases roosts where it builds, and the wood thrush occupies, as it were, the first story of the woods.

There is something singular about the distribution of the wood thrushes. At an earlier stage of my observations I should have been much surprised at finding them in these woods. Indeed, I had stated in print on two occasions that the wood thrush was not found in the higher lands of the Catskills, but that the hermit thrush and the veery, or Wilson's thrush, were common. It turns out that the statement is only half true. The wood thrush is found also, but is much more rare and secluded in its habits than either of the others, being seen only during the breeding season on remote mountains, and then only on their eastern and southern slopes. I have never yet in this region found the bird spending the season in the near and familiar woods, which is directly contrary to observations I have made in other parts of the State. So different are the habits of birds in different localities.

As soon as it was fairly light we were up and ready to resume our march. A small bit of bread and butter and a swallow or two of whiskey was all we had for breakfast that morning. Our supply of each was very limited, and we were anxious to save a little of both, to relieve the diet of trout to which we looked forward.

At an early hour we reached the rock where we had parted with the guide, and looked around us into the dense, trackless woods with many misgivings. To strike out now on our own hook, where the way was so blind and after the experience we had just had, was a step not to be carelessly taken. The tops of these mountains are so broad, and a short distance in the woods seems so far, that one is by no means master of the situation after reaching the summit. And then there are so many spurs and offshoots and changes of direction, added to the impossibility of making any generalization by the aid of the eye, that before one is aware of it he is very wide of his mark.

I remembered now that a young farmer of my acquaintance had told me how he had made a long day's march through the heart of this region, without path or guide of any kind, and had hit his mark squarely. He had been barkpeeling in Callikoon, — a famous country for bark, — and, having got enough of it, he desired to reach his home on Dry Brook without making the usual circuitous journey between the two places. To do this necessitated a march of ten or twelve miles across several ranges of mountains and through an unbroken forest, — a hazardous undertaking in which no one would join him. Even the old hunters who were familiar with the ground dissuaded him and predicted the failure of his enterprise. But having made up his mind, he possessed himself thoroughly of the topography of the country from the aforesaid hunters, shouldered his axe, and set out, holding a straight course through the woods, and turning aside for neither swamps, streams, nor mountains. When he paused to rest he would mark some object ahead of him with his eye, in order that on getting up again he might not deviate from his course. His directors had told him of a hunter's cabin about midway on his route, which if he struck he might be sure he was right. About noon this cabin was reached, and at sunset he emerged at the head of Dry Brook.

After looking in vain for the line of marked trees, we moved off to the left in a doubtful, hesitating manner, keeping on the highest ground and blazing the trees as we went. We were afraid to go downhill, lest we should descend too soon; our vantage-ground was high ground. A thick fog coming on, we were more bewildered than ever. Still we pressed forward, climbing up ledges and wading through ferns for about two hours, when we paused by a spring that issued from beneath an immense wall of rock that belted the highest part of the mountain. There was quite a broad plateau here, and the birch wood was very dense, and the trees of unusual size.

After resting and exchanging opinions, we all concluded that it was best not to continue our search encumbered as we were; but we were not willing to abandon it altogether, and I proposed to my companions to leave them beside the spring with our traps, while I made one thorough and final effort to find the lake. If I succeeded and desired them to come forward, I was to fire my gun three times; if I failed and wished to return, I would fire it twice, they of course responding.

So, filling my canteen from the spring, I set out again, taking the spring run for my guide. Before I had followed it two hundred yards, it sank into the ground at my feet. I had half a mind to be superstitious and to believe that we were under a spell, since our guides played us such tricks. However, I determined to put the matter to a further test, and struck out boldly to the left. This seemed to be the keyword, — to the left, to the left. The fog had now lifted, so that I could form a better idea of the lay of the land. Twice I looked down the steep sides of the mountain, sorely tempted to risk a plunge. Still I hesitated and kept along on the brink. As I stood on a rock deliberating, I heard a crackling of the brush, like the tread of some large game, on a plateau below me. Suspecting the truth of the case, I moved stealthily down, and found a herd of young cattle leisurely browsing. We had several times crossed their trail, and had seen that morning a level, grassy place on the top of the mountain, where they had passed the night. Instead of being frightened, as I had expected, they seemed greatly delighted, and gathered around me as if to inquire the tidings from the outer world, — perhaps the quotations of the cattle market. They came up to me, and eagerly licked my hand, clothes, and gun. Salt was what they were after, and they were ready to swallow anything that contained the smallest percentage of it. They were mostly yearlings and as sleek as moles. They had a very gamy look. We were afterwards told that, in the spring, the farmers round about turn into these woods their young cattle, which do not come out again till fall. They are then in good condition, — not fat, like grass-fed cattle, but trim and supple, like deer. Once a month the owner hunts them up and salts them. They have their beats, and seldom wander beyond well-defined limits. It was interesting to see them feed. They browsed on the low limbs and bushes, and on the various plants, munching at everything without any apparent discrimination.

They attempted to follow me, but I escaped them by clambering down some steep rocks. I now found myself gradually edging down the side of the mountain, keeping around it in a spiral manner, and scanning the woods and the shape of the ground for some encouraging hint or sign. Finally the woods became more open, and the descent less rapid. The trees were remarkably straight and uniform in size. Black birches, the first I had seen, were very numerous. I felt encouraged. Listening attentively, I caught, from a breeze just lifting the drooping leaves, a sound that I willingly believed was made by a bullfrog. On this hint, I tore down through the woods at my highest speed. Then I paused and listened again. This time there was no mistaking it; it was the sound of frogs. Much elated, I rushed on. By and by I could hear them as I ran. *Pthrung, pthrung,* croaked the old ones; *pug, pug,* shrilly joined in the smaller fry.

Then I caught, through the lower trees, a gleam of blue, which I first thought was distant sky. A second look and I knew it to be water, and in a moment more I stepped from the woods and stood upon the shore of the lake. I exulted silently. There it was at last, sparkling in the morning sun, and as beautiful as a dream. It was so good to come upon such open space and such bright hues, after wandering in the dim, dense woods! The eye is as delighted as an escaped bird, and darts gleefully from point to point.

The lake was a long oval, scarcely more than a mile in circumference, with evenly wooded shores, which rose gradually on all sides. After contemplating the scene for a moment, I stepped back into the woods, and, loading my gun as heavily as I dared, discharged it three times. The reports seemed to fill all the mountains with sound. The frogs quickly hushed, and I listened for the response. But no response came. Then I tried again and again, but without evoking an answer. One of my companions, however, who had climbed to the top of the high rocks in the rear of the spring, thought he heard faintly one report. It seemed an immense distance below him, and far around under the mountain. I knew I had come a long way, and hardly expected to be able to communicate with

188

my companions in the manner agreed upon. I
therefore started back, choosing my course without
any reference to the circuitous route by which I had
come, and loading heavily and firing at intervals.
I must have aroused many long-dormant echoes
from a Rip Van Winkle sleep. As my powder got
low, I fired and hallooed alternately, till I came near
splitting both my throat and gun. Finally, after I
had begun to have a very ugly feeling of alarm and
disappointment, and to cast about vaguely for some
course to pursue in the emergency that seemed near
at hand, — namely, the loss of my companions now
I had found the lake, — a favoring breeze brought
me the last echo of a response. I rejoined with
spirit, and hastened with all speed in the direction
whence the sound had come, but, after repeated trials, failed to elicit another answering sound. This
filled me with apprehension again. I feared that
my friends had been misled by the reverberations,
and I pictured them to myself hastening in the
opposite direction. Paying little attention to my
course, but paying dearly for my carelessness afterward, I rushed forward to undeceive them. But
they had not been deceived, and in a few moments an answering shout revealed them near at
hand. I heard their tramp, the bushes parted, and
we three met again.

In answer to their eager inquiries, I assured them
that I had seen the lake, that it was at the foot of

the mountain, and that we could not miss it if we kept straight down from where we then were.

My clothes were soaked with perspiration, but I shouldered my knapsack with alacrity, and we began the descent. I noticed that the woods were much thicker, and had quite a different look from those I had passed through, but thought nothing of it, as I expected to strike the lake near its head, whereas I had before come out at its foot. We had not gone far when we crossed a line of marked trees, which my companions were disposed to follow. It intersected our course nearly at right angles, and kept along and up the side of the mountain. My impression was that it led up from the lake, and that by keeping our own course we should reach the lake sooner than if we followed this line.

About halfway down the mountain, we could see through the interstices the opposite slope. I encouraged my comrades by telling them that the lake was between us and that, and not more than half a mile distant. We soon reached the bottom, where we found a small stream and quite an extensive alder swamp, evidently the ancient bed of a lake. I explained to my half-vexed and half-incredulous companions that we were probably above the lake, and that this stream must lead to it. "Follow it," they said ; "we will wait here till we hear from you."

So I went on, more than ever disposed to believe

that we were under a spell, and that the lake had
slipped from my grasp after all. Seeing no favorable sign as I went forward, I laid down my accoutrements, and climbed a decayed beech that leaned
out over the swamp and promised a good view from
the top. As I stretched myself up to look around
from the highest attainable branch, there was suddenly a loud crack at the root. With a celerity
that would at least have done credit to a bear, I
regained the ground, having caught but a momentary glimpse of the country, but enough to convince
me no lake was near. Leaving all incumbrances
here but my gun, I still pressed on, loath to be thus
baffled. After floundering through another alder
swamp for nearly half a mile, I flattered myself
that I was close on to the lake. I caught sight of
a low spur of the mountain sweeping around like
a half-extended arm, and I fondly imagined that
within its clasp was the object of my search. But
I found only more alder swamp. After this region
was cleared, the creek began to descend the mountain very rapidly. Its banks became high and nar-
row, and it went whirling away with a sound that
seemed to my ears like a burst of ironical laughter. I turned back with a feeling of mingled disgust, shame, and vexation. In fact I was almost
sick, and when I reached my companions, after an
absence of nearly two hours, hungry, fatigued, and
disheartened, I would have sold my interest in

Thomas's Lake at a very low figure. For the first time, I heartily wished myself well out of the woods. Thomas might keep his lake, and the enchanters guard his possession! I doubted if he had ever found it the second time, or if any one else ever had.

My companions, who were quite fresh, and who had not felt the strain of baffled purpose as I had, assumed a more encouraging tone. After I had rested awhile, and partaken sparingly of the bread and whiskey, which in such an emergency is a great improvement on bread and water, I agreed to their proposition that we should make another attempt. As if to reassure us, a robin sounded his cheery call near by, and the winter wren, the first I had heard in these woods, set his music-box going, which fairly ran over with fine, gushing, lyrical sounds. There can be no doubt but this bird is one of our finest songsters. If it would only thrive and sing well when caged, like the canary, how far it would surpass that bird! It has all the vivacity and versatility of the canary, without any of its shrillness. Its song is indeed a little cascade of melody.

We again retraced our steps, rolling the stone, as it were, back up the mountain, determined to commit ourselves to the line of marked trees. These we finally reached, and, after exploring the country to the right, saw that bearing to the left was still the order. The trail led up over a gentle rise of ground, and in less than twenty minutes we were in the woods I had passed through when I found the lake. The error I had made was then plain : we had come off the mountain a few paces too far to the right, and so had passed down on the wrong side of the ridge, into what we afterwards learned was the valley of Alder Creek.

We now made good time, and before many minutes I again saw the mimic sky glance through the trees. As we approached the lake, a solitary woodchuck, the first wild animal we had seen since entering the woods, sat crouched upon the root of a tree a few feet from the water, apparently completely nonplused by the unexpected appearance of danger on the land side. All retreat was cut off, and he looked his fate in the face without flinching. I slaughtered him just as a savage would have done, and from the same motive, — I wanted his carcass to eat.

The mid-afternoon sun was now shining upon the lake, and a low, steady breeze drove the little waves rocking to the shore. A herd of cattle were browsing on the other side, and the bell of the leader sounded across the water. In these solitudes its clang was wild and musical.

To try the trout was the first thing in order. On a rude raft of logs which we found moored at the shore, and which with two aboard shipped about a foot of water, we floated out and wet our first fly in Thomas's Lake; but the trout refused to jump,

193

and, to be frank, not more than a dozen and a half were caught during our stay. Only a week previous, a party of three had taken in a few hours all the fish they could carry out of the woods, and had nearly surfeited their neighbors with trout. But from some cause they now refused to rise, or to touch any kind of bait: so we fell to catching the sunfish, which were small but very abundant. Their nests were all along shore. A space about the size of a breakfast-plate was cleared of sediment and decayed vegetable matter, revealing the pebbly bottom, fresh and bright, with one or two fish suspended over the centre of it, keeping watch and ward. If an intruder approached, they would dart at him spitefully. These fish have the air of bantam cocks, and, with their sharp, prickly fins and spines and scaly sides, must be ugly customers in a hand-to-hand encounter with other finny warriors. To a hungry man they look about as unpromising as hemlock slivers, so thorny and thin are they; yet there is sweet meat in them, as we found that day.

Much refreshed, I set out with the sun low in the west to explore the outlet of the lake and try for trout there, while my companions made further trials in the lake itself. The outlet, as is usual in bodies of water of this kind, was very gentle and private. The stream, six or eight feet wide, flowed silently and evenly along for a distance of three or four rods, when it suddenly, as if conscious of

its freedom. took a leap down some rocks. Thence,
as far as I followed it, its descent was very rapid
through a continuous succession of brief falls like
so many steps down the mountain. Its appearance
promised more trout than I found, though I returned to camp with a very respectable string.

Toward sunset I went round to explore the inlet,
and found that as usual the stream wound leisurely
through marshy ground. The water being much
colder than in the outlet, the trout were more plentiful. As I was picking my way over the miry
ground and through the rank growths, a ruffed
grouse hopped up on a fallen branch a few paces
before me, and, jerking his tail, threatened to take
flight. But as I was at that moment gunless and
remained stationary, he presently jumped down and
walked away.

A seeker of birds, and ever on the alert for some
new acquaintance, my attention was arrested, on
first entering the swamp, by a bright, lively song,
or warble, that issued from the branches overhead,
and that was entirely new to me, though there was
something in the tone of it that told me the bird
was related to the wood-wagtail and to the water-
wagtail or thrush. The strain was emphatic and
quite loud, like the canary's, but very brief. The
bird kept itself well secreted in the upper branches
of the trees, and for a long time eluded my eye. I
passed to and fro several times, and it seemed to

break out afresh as I approached a certain little bend in the creek, and to cease after I had got beyond it; no doubt its nest was somewhere in the vicinity. After some delay the bird was sighted and brought down. It proved to be the small, or northern, water-thrush (called also the New York water-thrush), — a new bird to me. In size it was noticeably smaller than the large, or Louisiana, water-thrush, as described by Audubon, but in other respects its general appearance was the same. It was a great treat to me, and again I felt myself in luck.

This bird was unknown to the older ornithologists, and is but poorly described by the new. It builds a mossy nest on the ground, or under the edge of a decayed log. A correspondent writes me that he has found it breeding on the mountains in Pennsylvania. The large-billed water-thrush is much the superior songster, but the present species has a very bright and cheerful strain. The specimen I saw, contrary to the habits of the family, kept in the treetops like a warbler, and seemed to be engaged in catching insects.

The birds were unusually plentiful and noisy about the head of this lake; robins, blue jays, and woodpeckers greeted me with their familiar notes. The blue jays found an owl or some wild animal a short distance above me, and, as is their custom on such occasions, proclaimed it at the top of their voices, and kept on till the darkness began to gather in the woods.

I also heard here, as I had at two or three other points in the course of the day, the peculiar, reso- nant hammering of some species of woodpecker upon the hard, dry limbs. It was unlike any sound of the kind I had ever before heard, and, repeated at intervals through the silent woods, was a very marked and characteristic feature. Its peculiarity was the ordered succession of the raps, which gave it the character of a premeditated performance. There were first three strokes following each other rapidly, then two much louder ones with longer intervals between them. I heard the drumming here, and the next day at sunset at Furlow Lake, the source of Dry Brook, and in no instance was the order varied. There was melody in it, such as a wood- pecker knows how to evoke from a smooth, dry branch. It suggested something quite as pleasing as the liveliest bird-song, and was if anything more woodsy and wild. As the yellow-bellied woodpecker was the most abundant species in these woods, I attributed it to him. It is the one sound that still links itself with those scenes in my mind.

At sunset the grouse began to drum in all parts of the woods about the lake. I could hear five at one time, *thump, thump, thump, thump, thr-r-r- r-r-r-rr.* It was a homely, welcome sound. As I returned to camp at twilight, along the shore of the

197

lake, the frogs also were in full chorus. The older ones ripped out their responses to each other with terrific force and volume. I know of no other animal capable of giving forth so much sound, in proportion to its size, as a frog. Some of these seemed to bellow as loud as a two-year-old bull. They were of immense size, and very abundant. No frog-eater had ever been there. Near the shore we felled a tree which reached far out in the lake. Upon the trunk and branches the frogs soon collected in large numbers, and gamboled and splashed about the half-submerged top, like a parcel of schoolboys, making nearly as much noise.

After dark, as I was frying the fish, a panful of the largest trout was accidently capsized in the fire. With rueful countenances we contemplated the irreparable loss our commissariat had sustained by this mishap; but remembering there was virtue in ashes, we poked the half-consumed fish from the bed of coals and ate them, and they were good.

We lodged that night on a brush-heap and slept soundly. The green, yielding beech-twigs, covered with a buffalo robe, were equal to a hair mattress. The heat and smoke from a large fire kindled in the afternoon had banished every "no-see-em" from the locality, and in the morning the sun was above the mountain before we awoke.

I immediately started again for the inlet, and went far up the stream toward its source. A fair

string of trout for breakfast was my reward. The
cattle with the bell were at the head of the valley,
where they had passed the night. Most of them
were two-year-old steers. They came up to me and
begged for salt, and scared the fish by their impor-
tunities.

We finished our bread that morning, and ate
every fish we could catch, and about ten o'clock
prepared to leave the lake. The weather had been
admirable, and the lake was a gem, and I would
gladly have spent a week in the neighborhood; but
the question of supplies was a serious one, and
would brook no delay.

When we reached, on our return, the point where
we had crossed the line of marked trees the day
before, the question arose whether we should still
trust ourselves to this line, or follow our own trail
back to the spring and the battlement of rocks on
the top of the mountain, and thence to the rock
where the guide had left us. We decided in favor
of the former course. After a march of three quarters of an hour the blazed trees ceased, and we
concluded we were near the point at which we had
parted with the guide. So we built a fire, laid
down our loads, and cast about on all sides for some
clew as to our exact locality. Nearly an hour was
consumed in this manner, and without any result.
I came upon a brood of young grouse, which di-
verted me for a moment. The old one blustered

about at a furious rate, trying to draw all attention to herself, while the young ones, which were unable to fly, hid themselves. She whined like a dog in great distress, and dragged herself along apparently with the greatest difficulty. As I pursued her, she ran very nimbly, and presently flew a few yards. Then, as I went on, she flew farther and farther each time, till at last she got up, and went humming through the woods as if she had no interest in them. I went back and caught one of the young, which had simply squatted close to the leaves. I took it up and set it on the palm of my hand, which it hugged as closely as if still upon the ground. I then put it in my coatsleeve, when it ran and nestled in my armpit.

When we met at the sign of the smoke, opinions differed as to the most feasible course. There was no doubt but that we could get out of the woods; but we wished to get out speedily, and as near as possible to the point where we had entered. Half ashamed of our timidity and indecision, we finally tramped away back to where we had crossed the line of blazed trees, followed our old trail to the spring on the top of the range, and, after much searching and scouring to the right and left, found ourselves at the very place we had left two hours before. Another deliberation and a divided council. But something must be done. It was then mid-afternoon, and the prospect of spending another night

on the mountains, without food or drink, was not
pleasant. So we moved down the ridge. Here
another line of marked trees was found, the course
of which formed an obtuse angle with the one we
had followed. It kept on the top of the ridge for
perhaps a mile, when it entirely disappeared, and
we were as much adrift as ever. Then one of the
party swore an oath, and said he was going out of
those woods, hit or miss, and, wheeling to the right,
instantly plunged over the brink of the mountain.
The rest followed, but would fain have paused and
ciphered away at their own uncertainties, to see if
a certainty could not be arrived at as to where we
would come out. But our bold leader was solving
the problem in the right way. Down and down
and still down we went, as if we were to bring up
in the bowels of the earth. It was by far the steepest
descent we had made, and we felt a grim satisfaction in knowing that we could not retrace our steps
this time, be the issue what it might. As we paused
on the brink of a ledge of rocks, we chanced to see
through the trees distant cleared land. A house
or barn also was dimly descried. This was encouraging ; but we could not make out whether
it was on Beaver Kill or Mill Brook or Dry Brook,
and did not long stop to consider where it was.
We at last brought up at the bottom of a deep
gorge, through which flowed a rapid creek that
literally swarmed with trout. But we were in no

mood to catch them, and pushed on along the channel of the stream, sometimes leaping from rock to rock, and sometimes splashing heedlessly through the water, and speculating the while as to where we should probably come out. On the Beaver Kill, my companions thought; but, from the position of the sun, I said, on the Mill Brook, about six miles below our team; for I remembered having seen, in coming up this stream, a deep, wild valley that led up into the mountains, like this one. Soon the banks of the stream became lower, and we moved into the woods. Here we entered upon an obscure wood-road, which presently conducted us into the midst of a vast hemlock forest. The land had a gentle slope, and we wondered why the lumbermen and barkmen who prowl through these woods had left this fine tract untouched. Beyond this the forest was mostly birch and maple.

We were now close to the settlement, and began to hear human sounds. One rod more, and we were out of the woods. It took us a moment to comprehend the scene. Things looked very strange at first; but quickly they began to change and to put on familiar features. Some magic scene-shifting seemed to take place before my eyes, till, instead of the unknown settlement which I at first seemed to look upon, there stood the farmhouse at which we had stopped two days before, and at the same moment we heard the stamping of our team in

BIRCH BROWSINGS

the barn. We sat down and laughed heartily over our good luck. Our desperate venture had resulted better than we had dared to hope, and had shamed our wisest plans. At the house our arrival had been anticipated about this time, and dinner was being put upon the table.

It was then five o'clock, so that we had been in the woods just forty-eight hours; but if time is only phenomenal, as the philosophers say, and life only in feeling, as the poets aver, we were some months, if not years, older at that moment than we had been two days before. Yet younger, too, — though this be a paradox, — for the birches had infused into us some of their own suppleness and strength.

1869.

VII

THE BLUEBIRD

WHEN Nature made the bluebird she wished to propitiate both the sky and the earth, so she gave him the color of the one on his back and the hue of the other on his breast, and ordained that his appearance in spring should denote that the strife and war between these two elements was at an end. He is the peace-harbinger; in him the celestial and terrestrial strike hands and are fast friends. He means the furrow and he means the warmth; he means all the soft, wooing influences of the spring on the one hand, and the retreating footsteps of winter on the other.

It is sure to be a bright March morning when you first hear his note; and it is as if the milder influences up above had found a voice and let a word fall upon your ear, so tender is it and so prophetic, a hope tinged with a regret.

"*Bermuda! Bermuda! Bermuda!*" he seems to say, as if both invoking and lamenting, and, behold! Bermuda follows close, though the little pilgrim may be only repeating the tradition of his race, himself having come only from Florida, the

205

Carolinas, or even from Virginia, where he has
found his Bermuda on some broad sunny hillside
thickly studded with cedars and persimmon-trees.

In New York and in New England the sap starts
up in the sugar maple the very day the bluebird
arrives, and sugar-making begins forthwith. The
bird is generally a mere disembodied voice; a rumor
in the air for two or three days before it takes visible shape before you. The males are the pioneers,
and come several days in advance of the females.
By the time both are here and the pairs have begun
to prospect for a place to nest, sugar-making is
over, the last vestige of snow has disappeared, and
the plow is brightening its mould-board in the new
furrow.

The bluebird enjoys the preëminence of being the
first bit of color that cheers our northern landscape.
The other birds that arrive about the same time —
the sparrow, the robin, the phœbe-bird — are clad
in neutral tints, gray, brown, or russet; but the
bluebird brings one of the primary hues and the
divinest of them all.

This bird also has the distinction of answering
very nearly to the robin redbreast of English memory, and was by the early settlers of New England
christened the blue robin.

It is a size or two larger, and the ruddy hue of
its breast does not verge so nearly on an orange, but
the manners and habits of the two birds are very

Bluebird

much alike. Our bird has the softer voice, but the English redbreast is much the more skilled musician. He has indeed a fine, animated warble, heard nearly the year through about English gardens and along the old hedge-rows, that is quite beyond the compass of our bird's instrument. On the other hand, our bird is associated with the spring as the British species cannot be, being a winter resident also, while the brighter sun and sky of the New World have given him a coat that far surpasses that of his transatlantic cousin.

It is worthy of remark that among British birds there is no *blue* bird. The cerulean tint seems much rarer among the feathered tribes there than here. On this continent there are at least three species of the common bluebird, while in all our woods there is the blue jay and the indigo-bird, — the latter so intensely blue as to fully justify its name. There is also the blue grosbeak, not much behind the indigo-bird in intensity of color; and among our warblers the blue tint is very common.

It is interesting to know that the bluebird is not confined to any one section of the country; and that when one goes West he will still have this favorite with him, though a little changed in voice and color, just enough to give variety without marring the identity.

The Western bluebird is considered a distinct species, and is perhaps a little more brilliant and showy than its Eastern brother; and Nuttall thinks its song is more varied, sweet, and tender. Its color approaches to ultramarine, while it has a sash of chestnut-red across its shoulders, — all the effects, I suspect, of that wonderful air and sky of California, and of those great Western plains; or, if one goes a little higher up into the mountainous regions of the West, he finds the Arctic bluebird, the ruddy brown on the breast changed to greenish blue, and the wings longer and more pointed; in other respects not differing much from our species.

The bluebird usually builds its nest in a hole in a stump or stub, or in an old cavity excavated by a woodpecker, when such can be had; but its first impulse seems to be to start in the world in much more style, and the happy pair make a great show of house-hunting about the farm buildings, now half persuaded to appropriate a dove-cote, then discussing in a lively manner a last year's swallow's nest, or proclaiming with much flourish and flutter that they have taken the wren's house, or the tenement of the purple martin; till finally nature becomes too urgent, when all this pretty make-believe ceases, and most of them settle back upon the old family stumps and knotholes in remote fields, and go to work in earnest.

In such situations the female is easily captured by approaching very stealthily and covering the entrance to the nest. The bird seldom makes any effort to escape, seeing how hopeless the case is, and keeps her place on the nest till she feels your hand closing around her. I have looked down into the cavity and seen the poor thing palpitating with fear and looking up with distended eyes, but never moving till I had withdrawn a few paces; then she rushes out with a cry that brings the male on the scene in a hurry. He warbles and lifts his wings beseechingly, but shows no anger or disposition to scold and complain like most birds. Indeed, this bird seems incapable of uttering a harsh note, or of doing a spiteful, ill-tempered thing.

The ground-builders all have some art or device to decoy one away from the nest, affecting lameness, a crippled wing, or a broken back, promising an easy capture if pursued. The tree-builders depend upon concealing the nest or placing it beyond reach. But the bluebird has no art either way, and its nest is easily found.

About the only enemies the sitting bird or the nest is in danger of are snakes and squirrels. I knew of a farm-boy who was in the habit of putting his hand down into a bluebird's nest and taking out the old bird whenever he came that way. One day he put his hand in, and, feeling something peculiar, withdrew it hastily, when it was instantly followed by the head and neck of an enormous black snake. The boy took to his heels and the snake gave chase.

pressing him close till a plowman near by came to the rescue with his ox-whip.

There never was a happier or more devoted husband than the male bluebird is. But among nearly all our familiar birds the serious cares of life seem to devolve almost entirely upon the female. The male is hilarious and demonstrative, the female serious and anxious about her charge. The male is the attendant of the female, following her wherever she goes. He never leads, never directs, but only seconds and applauds. If his life is all poetry and romance, hers is all business and prose. She has no pleasure but her duty, and no duty but to look after her nest and brood. She shows no affection for the male, no pleasure in his society; she only tolerates him as a necessary evil, and, if he is killed, goes in quest of another in the most business-like manner, as you would go for the plumber or the glazier. In most cases the male is the ornamental partner in the firm, and contributes little of the working capital. There seems to be more equality of the sexes among the woodpeckers, wrens, and swallows; while the contrast is greatest, perhaps, in the bobolink family, where the courting is done in the Arab fashion, the female fleeing with all her speed and the male pursuing with equal precipitation; and were it not for the broods of young birds that appear, it would be hard to believe that the intercourse ever ripened into anything more intimate.

THE BLUEBIRD

With the bluebirds the male is useful as well as ornamental. He is the gay champion and escort of the female at all times, and while she is sitting he feeds her regularly. It is very pretty to watch them building their nest. The male is very active in hunting out a place and exploring the boxes and cavities, but seems to have no choice in the matter and is anxious only to please and encourage his mate, who has the practical turn and knows what will do and what will not. After she has suited herself he applauds her immensely, and away the two go in quest of material for the nest, the male acting as guard and flying above and in advance of the female. She brings all the material and does all the work of building, he looking on and encouraging her with gesture and song. He acts also as inspector of her work, but I fear is a very partial one. She enters the nest with her bit of dry grass or straw, and, having adjusted it to her notion, withdraws and waits near by while he goes in and looks it over. On coming out he exclaims very plainly, "*Excellent! excellent!*" and away the two go again for more material.

The bluebirds, when they build about the farm buildings, sometimes come in conflict with the swallows. The past season I knew a pair to take forcible possession of the domicile of a pair of the latter, — the cliff species that now stick their nests under the eaves of the barn. The bluebirds had been broken up in a little bird-house near by, by the rats or perhaps a weasel, and being no doubt in a bad humor, and the season being well advanced, they made forcible entrance into the adobe tenement of their neighbors, and held possession of it for some days, but I believe finally withdrew, rather than live amid such a squeaky, noisy colony. I have heard that these swallows, when ejected from their homes in that way by the phœbe-bird, have been known to fall to and mason up the entrance to the nest while their enemy was inside of it, thus having a revenge as complete and cruel as anything in human annals.

The bluebirds and the house wrens more frequently come into collision. A few years ago I put up a little bird-house in the back end of my garden for the accommodation of the wrens, and every season a pair have taken up their abode there. One spring a pair of bluebirds looked into the tenement and lingered about several days, leading me to hope that they would conclude to occupy it. But they finally went away, and later in the season the wrens appeared, and, after a little coquetting, were regularly installed in their old quarters, and were as happy as only wrens can be.

One of our younger poets, Myron Benton, saw a little bird

" Ruffled with whirlwind of his ecstasies,"

which must have been the wren, as I know of no
other bird that so throbs and palpitates with music
as this little vagabond. And the pair I speak of
seemed exceptionally happy, and the male had a
small tornado of song in his crop that kept him
"ruffled" every moment in the day. But before
their honeymoon was over the bluebirds returned.
I knew something was wrong before I was up in
the morning. Instead of that voluble and gushing
song outside the window, I heard the wrens scolding and crying at a fearful rate, and on going out
saw the bluebirds in possession of the box. The
poor wrens were in despair; they wrung their hands
and tore their hair, after the wren fashion, but
chiefly did they rattle out their disgust and wrath
at the intruders. I have no doubt that, if it could
have been interpreted, it would have proven the
rankest and most voluble Billingsgate ever uttered.
For the wren is saucy, and he has a tongue in his
head that can outwag any other tongue known to me.

The bluebirds said nothing, but the male kept
an eye on Mr. Wren ; and, when he came too near,
gave chase, driving him to cover under the fence,
or under a rubbish-heap or other object, where the
wren would scold and rattle away, while his pursuer
sat on the fence or the pea-brush waiting for him to
reappear.

Days passed, and the usurpers prospered and the
outcasts were wretched ; but the latter lingered

about, watching and abusing their enemies, and hoping, no doubt, that things would take a turn, as they presently did. The outraged wrens were fully avenged. The mother bluebird had laid her full complement of eggs and was beginning to set, when one day, as her mate was perched above her on the barn, along came a boy with one of those wicked elastic slings and cut him down with a pebble. There he lay like a bit of sky fallen upon the grass. The widowed bird seemed to understand what had happened, and without much ado disappeared next day in quest of another mate. How she contrived to make her wants known, without trumpeting them about, I am unable to say. But I presume the birds have a way of advertising that answers the purpose well. Maybe she trusted to luck to fall in with some stray bachelor or bereaved male who would undertake to console a widow of one day's standing. I will say, in passing, that there are no bachelors from choice among the birds; they are all rejected suitors, while old maids are entirely unknown. There is a Jack to every Jill; and some to boot.

The males, being more exposed by their song and plumage, and by being the pioneers in migrating, seem to be slightly in excess lest the supply fall short, and hence it sometimes happens that a few are bachelors perforce; there are not females enough to go around, but before the season is over there are sure to be some vacancies in the marital ranks, which they are called on to fill.

In the mean time the wrens were beside themselves with delight; they fairly screamed with joy. If the male was before "ruffled with whirlwind of his ecstasies," he was now in danger of being rent asunder. He inflated his throat and caroled as wren never caroled before. And the female, too, how she cackled and darted about! How busy they both were! Rushing into the nest, they hustled those eggs out in less than a minute, wren time. They carried in new material, and by the third day were fairly installed again in their old quarters; but on the third day, so rapidly are these little dramas played, the female bluebird reappeared with another mate. Ah! how the wren stock went down then! What dismay and despair filled again those little breasts! It was pitiful. They did not scold as before, but after a day or two withdrew from the garden, dumb with grief, and gave up the struggle.

The bluebird, finding her eggs gone and her nest changed, seemed suddenly seized with alarm and shunned the box; or else, finding she had less need for another husband than she thought, repented her rashness and wanted to dissolve the compact. But the happy bridegroom would not take the hint, and exerted all his eloquence to comfort and reassure her. He was fresh and fond, and until this bereaved female found him I am sure his suit had not prospered that season. He thought the box just the thing, and that there was no need of alarm, and spent days in trying to persuade the female back. Seeing he could not be a stepfather to a family, he was quite willing to assume a nearer relation. He hovered about the box, he went in and out, he called, he warbled, he entreated; the female would respond occasionally and come and alight near, and even peep into the nest, but would not enter it, and quickly flew away again. Her mate would reluctantly follow, but he was soon back, uttering the most confident and cheering calls. If she did not come he would perch above the nest and sound his loudest notes over and over again, looking in the direction of his mate and beckoning with every motion. But she responded less and less frequently. Some days I would see him only, but finally he gave it up; the pair disappeared, and the box remained deserted the rest of the summer.

1867.

VIII

THE INVITATION

YEARS ago, when quite a youth, I was rambling in the woods one Sunday, with my brothers, gathering black birch, wintergreens, etc., when, as we reclined upon the ground, gazing vaguely up into the trees, I caught sight of a bird, that paused a moment on a branch above me, the like of which I had never before seen or heard of. It was probably the blue yellow-backed warbler, as I have since found this to be a common bird in those woods; but to my young fancy it seemed like some fairy bird, so curiously marked was it, and so new and unexpected. I saw it a moment as the flickering leaves parted, noted the white spot on its wing, and it was gone. How the thought of it clung to me afterward! It was a revelation. It was the first intimation I had had that the woods we knew so well held birds that we knew not at all. Were our eyes and ears so dull, then? There was the robin, the blue jay, the bluebird, the yellowbird, the cherry-bird, the catbird, the chippingbird, the woodpecker, the high-hole, an occasional redbird, and a few others, in the woods or along

217

their borders, but who ever dreamed that there were still others that not even the hunters saw, and whose names no one had ever heard?

When, one summer day, later in life, I took my gun and went to the woods again, in a different though perhaps a less simple spirit I found my youthful vision more than realized. There were, indeed, other birds, plenty of them, singing, nesting, breeding, among the familiar trees, which I had before passed by unheard and unseen.

It is a surprise that awaits every student of ornithology, and the thrill of delight that accompanies it, and the feeling of fresh, eager inquiry that follows, can hardly be awakened by any other pursuit. Take the first step in ornithology, procure one new specimen, and you are ticketed for the whole voyage. There is a fascination about it quite overpowering. It fits so well with other things,—with fishing, hunting, farming, walking, camping-out, — with all that takes one to the fields and woods. One may go a-blackberrying and make some rare discovery; or, while driving his cow to pasture, hear a new song, or make a new observation. Secrets lurk on all sides. There is news in every bush. Expectation is ever on tiptoe. What no man ever saw before may the next moment be revealed to you. What a new interest the woods have! How you long to explore every nook and corner of them! You would even find consolation in being lost in

them. You could then hear the night birds and
the owls, and, in your wanderings, might stumble
upon some unknown specimen.

In all excursions to the woods or to the shore,
the student of ornithology has an advantage over
his companions. He has one more resource, one
more avenue of delight. He, indeed, kills two
birds with one stone and sometimes three. If
others wander, he can never go out of his way.
His game is everywhere. The cawing of a crow
makes him feel at home, while a new note or a new
song drowns all care. Audubon, on the desolate
coast of Labrador, is happier than any king ever
was; and on shipboard is nearly cured of his sea-
sickness when a new gull appears in sight.

One must taste it to understand or appreciate its
fascination. The looker-on sees nothing to inspire
such enthusiasm. Only a few feathers and a half-
musical note or two; why all this ado? "Who
would give a hundred and twenty dollars to know
about the birds?" said an Eastern governor, half
contemptuously, to Wilson, as the latter solicited
a subscription to his great work. Sure enough.
Bought knowledge is dear at any price. The most
precious things have no commercial value. It is
not, your Excellency, mere technical knowledge of
the birds that you are asked to purchase, but a new
interest in the fields and woods, a new moral and
intellectual tonic, a new key to the treasure-house

of Nature. Think of the many other things your Excellency would get, — the air, the sunshine, the healing fragrance and coolness, and the many respites from the knavery and turmoil of political life.

Yesterday was an October day of rare brightness and warmth. I spent the most of it in a wild, wooded gorge of Rock Creek. A persimmon-tree which stood upon the bank had dropped some of its fruit in the water. As I stood there, half-leg deep, picking them up, a wood duck came flying down the creek and passed over my head. Presently it returned, flying up; then it came back again, and, sweeping low around a bend, prepared to alight in a still, dark reach in the creek which was hidden from my view. As I passed that way about half an hour afterward, the duck started up, uttering its wild alarm note. In the stillness I could hear the whistle of its wings and the splash of the water when it took flight. Near by I saw where a raccoon had come down to the water for fresh clams, leaving his long, sharp track in the mud and sand. Before I had passed this hidden stretch of water, a pair of those mysterious thrushes, the gray-cheeked, flew up from the ground and perched on a low branch.

Who can tell how much this duck, this footprint in the sand, and these strange thrushes from the far north, enhanced the interest and charm of the autumn woods?

THE INVITATION

Ornithology cannot be satisfactorily learned from the books. The satisfaction is in learning it from nature. One must have an original experience with the birds. The books are only the guide, the invitation. Though there remain not another new species to describe, any young person with health and enthusiasm has open to him or her the whole field anew, and is eligible to experience all the thrill and delight of original discoverers.

But let me say, in the same breath, that the books can by no manner of means be dispensed with. A copy of Wilson or Audubon, for reference and to compare notes with, is invaluable. In lieu of these, access to some large museum or collection would be a great help. In the beginning, one finds it very difficult to identify a bird from any verbal description. Reference to a colored plate, or to a stuffed specimen, at once settles the matter. This is the chief value of the books; they are charts to sail by; the route is mapped out, and much time and labor are thereby saved. First find your bird; observe its ways, its song, its calls, its flight, its haunts; then shoot it (not ogle it with a glass), and compare with Audubon.[1] In this way the feathered kingdom may soon be conquered.

The ornithologists divide and subdivide the birds into a great many orders, families, genera, species,

[1] My later experiences have led me to prefer a small field-glass to a gun.

etc., which, at first sight, are apt to confuse and discourage the reader. But any interested person can acquaint himself with most of our song-birds by keeping in mind a few general divisions, and observing the characteristics of each. By far the greater number of our land-birds are either warblers, vireos, flycatchers, thrushes, or finches.

The warblers are, perhaps, the most puzzling. These are the true Sylvia, the real wood-birds. They are small, very active, but feeble songsters, and, to be seen, must be sought for. In passing through the woods, most persons have a vague consciousness of slight chirping, semi-musical sounds in the trees overhead. In most cases these sounds proceed from the warblers. Throughout the Middle and Eastern States, half a dozen species or so may be found in almost every locality, as the redstart, the Maryland yellow-throat, the yellow warbler (not the common goldfinch, with black cap, and black wings and tail), the hooded warbler, the black and white creeping warbler; or others, according to the locality and the character of the woods. In pine or hemlock woods, one species may predominate; in maple or oak woods, or in mountainous districts, another. The subdivision of ground warblers, the most common members of which are the Maryland yellow-throat, the Kentucky warbler, and the mourning ground warbler, are usually found in low, wet, bushy, or half-open woods, often on and always near the ground. The summer yellowbird, or yellow warbler, is not now a wood-bird at all, being found in orchards and parks, and along streams and in the trees of villages and cities.

As we go north the number of warblers increases, till, in the northern part of New England, and in the Canadas, as many as ten or twelve varieties may be found breeding in June. Audubon found the black-poll warbler breeding in Labrador, and congratulates himself on being the first white man who had ever seen its nest. When these warblers pass north in May, they seem to go singly or in pairs, and their black caps and striped coats show conspicuously. When they return in September they are in troops or loose flocks, are of a uniform dull drab or brindlish color, and are very fat. They scour the treetops for a few days, almost eluding the eye by their quick movements, and are gone.

According to my own observation, the number of species of warblers which one living in the middle districts sees, on their return in the fall, is very small compared with the number he may observe migrating north in the spring.

The yellow-rumped warblers are the most noticeable of all in the autumn. They come about the streets and garden, and seem especially drawn to dry, leafless trees. They dart spitefully about, uttering a sharp chirp. In Washington I have seen them in the outskirts all winter.

Audubon figures and describes over forty different warblers. More recent writers have divided and subdivided the group very much, giving new names to new classifications. But this part is of interest and value only to the professional ornithologist.

The finest songster among the Sylvia, according to my notions, is the black-throated greenback. Its song is sweet and clear, but brief.

The rarest of the species are Swainson's warbler, said to be disappearing; the cerulean warbler, said to be abundant about Niagara; and the mourning ground warbler, which I have found breeding about the head-waters of the Delaware, in New York.

The vireos, or greenlets, are a sort of connecting link between the warblers and the true flycatchers, and partake of the characteristics of both.

The red-eyed vireo, whose sweet soliloquy is one of the most constant and cheerful sounds in our woods and groves, is perhaps the most noticeable and abundant species. The vireos are a little larger than the warblers, and are far less brilliant and variegated in color.

There are five species found in most of our woods, namely, the red-eyed vireo, the white-eyed vireo, the warbling vireo, the yellow-throated vireo, and the solitary vireo, — the red-eyed and warbling being most abundant, and the white-eyed being the most lively and animated songster. I meet the lat-

ter bird only in the thick, bushy growths of low,
swampy localities, where, eluding the observer, it
pours forth its song with a sharpness and a rapidity
of articulation that are truly astonishing. This
strain is very marked, and, though inlaid with the
notes of several other birds, is entirely unique. The
iris of this bird is white, as that of the red-eyed is
red, though in neither case can this mark be distinguished at more than two or three yards. In most
cases the iris of birds is a dark hazel, which passes
for black.

The basket-like nest, pendent to the low branches
in the woods, which the falling leaves of autumn
reveal to all passers, is, in most cases, the nest of
the red-eyed, though the solitary constructs a similar tenement, but in much more remote and secluded
localities.

Most birds exhibit great alarm and distress, usually with a strong dash of anger, when you approach
their nests; but the demeanor of the red-eyed, on
such an occasion, is an exception to this rule. The
parent birds move about softly amid the branches
above, eying the intruder with a curious, innocent
look, uttering, now and then, a subdued note or
plaint, solicitous and watchful, but making no de-
monstration of anger or distress.

The birds, no more than the animals, like to be
caught napping; but I remember, one autumn day,
coming upon a red-eyed vireo that was clearly

oblivious to all that was passing around it. It was a young bird, though full grown, and it was taking its siesta on a low branch in a remote heathery field. Its head was snugly stowed away under its wing, and it would have fallen an easy prey to the first hawk that came along. I approached noiselessly, and when within a few feet of it paused to note its breathings, so much more rapid and full than our own. A bird has greater lung capacity than any other living thing, hence more animal heat, and life at a higher pressure. When I reached out my hand and carefully closed it around the winged sleeper, its sudden terror and consternation almost paralyzed it. Then it struggled and cried piteously, and when released hastened and hid itself in some near bushes. I never expected to surprise it thus a second time.

The flycatchers are a larger group than the vireos, with stronger-marked characteristics. They are not properly songsters, but are classed by some writers as screechers. Their pugnacious dispositions are well known, and they not only fight among themselves, but are incessantly quarreling with their neighbors. The kingbird, or tyrant flycatcher, might serve as the type of the order.

The common or wood pewee excites the most pleasant emotions, both on account of its plaintive note and its exquisite mossy nest.

The phœbe-bird is the pioneer of the flycatchers,

and comes in April, sometimes in March. It comes familiarly about the house and outbuildings, and usually builds beneath hay-sheds or under bridges.

The flycatchers always take their insect prey on the wing, by a sudden darting or swooping movement; often a very audible snap of the beak may be heard.

These birds are the least elegant, both in form and color, of any of our feathered neighbors. They have short legs, a short neck, large heads, and broad, flat beaks, with bristles at the base. They often fly with a peculiar quivering movement of the wings, and when at rest some of the species oscillate their tails at short intervals.

There are found in the United States nineteen species. In the Middle and Eastern districts, one may observe in summer, without any special search, about five of them, namely, the kingbird, the phœbe-bird, the wood pewee, the great crested flycatcher (distinguished from all others by the bright ferruginous color of its tail), and the small green-crested flycatcher.

The thrushes are the birds of real melody, and will afford one more delight perhaps than any other class. The robin is the most familiar example. Their manners, flight, and form are the same in each species. See the robin hop along upon the ground, strike an attitude, scratch for a worm, fix his eye upon something before him or upon the beholder, flip his wings suspiciously, fly straight to his perch, or sit at sundown on some high branch caroling his sweet and honest strain, and you have seen what is characteristic of all the thrushes. Their carriage is preëminently marked by grace, and their songs by melody.

Beside the robin, which is in no sense a wood-bird, we have in New York the wood thrush, the hermit thrush, the veery, or Wilson's thrush, the olive-backed thrush, and, transiently, one or two other species not so clearly defined.

The wood thrush and the hermit stand at the head as songsters, no two persons, perhaps, agreeing as to which is the superior.

Under the general head of finches, Audubon describes over sixty different birds, ranging from the sparrows to the grosbeaks, and including the buntings, the linnets, the snowbirds, the crossbills, and the redbirds.

We have nearly or quite a dozen varieties of the sparrow in the Atlantic States, but perhaps no more than half that number would be discriminated by the unprofessional observer. The song sparrow, which every child knows, comes first; at least, his voice is first heard. And can there be anything more fresh and pleasing than this first simple strain heard from the garden fence or a near hedge, on some bright, still March morning?

The field or vesper sparrow, called also grass

finch and bay-winged sparrow, a bird slightly
larger than the song sparrow and of a lighter gray
color, is abundant in all our upland fields and pastures, and is a very sweet songster. It builds upon
the ground, without the slightest cover or protection, and also roosts there. Walking through the
fields at dusk, I frequently start them up almost
beneath my feet. When disturbed by day, they fly
with a quick, sharp movement, showing two white
quills in the tail. The traveler along the country roads disturbs them earthing their wings in the
soft dry earth, or sees them skulking and flitting
along the fences in front of him. They run in the
furrow in advance of the team, or perch upon the
stones a few rods off. They sing much after sundown, hence the aptness of the name vesper sparrow, which a recent writer, Wilson Flagg, has be-
stowed upon them.

In the meadows and low, wet lands the savanna
sparrow is met with, and may be known by its fine,
insect-like song; in the swamp, the swamp sparrow.

The fox sparrow, the largest and handsomest species of this family, comes to us in the fall, from
the North, where it breeds. Likewise the tree or
Canada sparrow, and the white-crowned and white-
throated sparrows.

The social sparrow, *alias* "hairbird," *alias* "red-
headed chipping-bird," is the smallest of the spar-

rows, and, I believe, the only one that builds in trees.

The finches, as a class, all have short conical bills, with tails more or less forked. The purple finch heads the list in varied musical ability.

Beside the groups of our more familiar birds which I have thus hastily outlined, there are numerous other groups, more limited in specimens but comprising some of our best-known songsters. The bobolink, for instance, has properly no congener. The famous mockingbird of the Southern States belongs to a genus which has but two other representatives in the Atlantic States, namely, the catbird and the long-tailed or ferruginous thrush.

The wrens are a large and interesting family, and as songsters are noted for vivacity and volubility. The more common species are the house wren, the marsh wren, the great Carolina wren, and the winter wren, the latter perhaps deriving its name from the fact that it breeds in the North. It is an exquisite songster, and pours forth its notes so rapidly, and with such sylvan sweetness and cadence, that it seems to *go off* like a musical alarm.

Wilson called the kinglets wrens, but they have little to justify the name, except that the ruby-crown's song is of the same gushing, lyrical character as that referred to above. Dr. Brewer was entranced with the song of one of these tiny minstrels in the woods of New Brunswick, and thought he ıad found the author of the strain in the black-poll warbler. He seems loath to believe that a bird so small as either of the kinglets could possess such vocal powers. It may indeed have been the winter wren, but from my own observation I believe the ruby-crowned kinglet quite capable of such a performance.

But I must leave this part of the subject and hasten on. As to works on ornithology, Audubon's, though its expense puts it beyond the reach of the mass of readers, is by far the most full and accurate. His drawings surpass all others in accuracy and spirit, while his enthusiasm and devotion to the work he had undertaken have but few parallels in the history of science. His chapter on the wild goose is as good as a poem. One readily overlooks his style, which is often verbose and affected, in consideration of enthusiasm so genuine and purpose so single.

There has never been a keener eye than Audubon's, though there have been more discriminative ears. Nuttall, for instance, is far more happy in his descriptions of the songs and notes of birds, and more to be relied upon. Audubon thinks the song of the Louisiana water-thrush equal to that of the European nightingale, and, as he had heard both birds, one would think was prepared to judge. Yet he has, no doubt, overrated the one and underrated the other. The song of the water-thrush is very

231

brief, compared with the philomel's, and its quality is brightness and vivacity, while that of the latter bird, if the books are to be credited, is melody and harmony. Again, he says the song of the blue grosbeak resembles the bobolink's, which it does about as much as the two birds resemble each other in color; one is black and white and the other is blue. The song of the wood-wagtail, he says, consists of a "short succession of simple notes beginning with emphasis and gradually falling." The truth is, they run up the scale instead of down, beginning low and ending in a shriek.

Yet, considering the extent of Audubon's work, the wonder is the errors are so few. I can at this moment recall but one observation of his, the contrary of which I have proved to be true. In his account of the bobolink he makes a point of the fact that, in returning south in the fall, they do not travel by night as they do when moving north in the spring. In Washington I have heard their calls as they flew over at night for four successive autumns. As he devoted the whole of a long life to the subject, and figured and described over four hundred species, one feels a real triumph on finding in our common woods a bird not described in his work. I have seen but two. Walking in the woods one day in early fall, in the vicinity of West Point, I started up a thrush that was sitting on the ground. It alighted on a branch a few yards off, and looked

new to me. I thought I had never before seen
so long-legged a thrush. I shot it, and saw that it
was a new acquaintance. Its peculiarities were its
broad, square tail; the length of its legs, which
were three and three quarters inches from the end
of the middle toe to the hip-joint; and the deep
uniform olive-brown of the upper parts, and the
gray of the lower. It proved to be the gray-cheeked
thrush, named and first described by Professor
Baird. But little seems to be known concerning it,
except that it breeds in the far north, even on the
shores of the Arctic Ocean. I would go a good way
to hear its song.

The present season I met with a pair of them
near Washington, as mentioned above. In size
this bird approaches the wood thrush, being larger
than either the hermit or the veery; unlike all
other species, no part of its plumage has a tawny
or yellowish tinge. The other specimen was the
northern or small water-thrush, cousin-german to
the oven-bird and half-brother to the Louisiana
water-thrush or wagtail. I found it at the head of
a remote mountain lake among the sources of the
Delaware, where it evidently had a nest. It usually
breeds much farther north. It has a strong, clear
warble, which at once suggests the song of its congener. I have not been able to find any account of
this particular species in the books, though it seems
to be well known.

More recent writers and explorers have added to
Audubon's list over three hundred new species, the
greater number of which belong to the northern
and western parts of the continent. Audubon's
observations were confined mainly to the Atlantic
and Gulf States and the adjacent islands; hence the
Western or Pacific birds were but little known to
him, and are only briefly mentioned in his works.

It is, by the way, a little remarkable how many
of the Western birds seem merely duplicates of the
Eastern. Thus, the varied thrush of the West is
our robin, a little differently marked; and the red-
shafted woodpecker is our golden-wing, or high-
hole, colored red instead of yellow. There is also a
Western chickadee, a Western chewink, a Western
blue jay, a Western meadowlark, a Western snowbird, a Western bluebird, a Western song sparrow,
Western grouse, quail, hen-hawk, etc.

One of the most remarkable birds of the West
seems to be a species of skylark, met with on the
plains of Dakota, which mounts to the height of
three or four hundred feet, and showers down its
ecstatic notes. It is evidently akin to several of
our Eastern species.

A correspondent, writing to me from the country
one September, said: "I have observed recently a
new species of bird here. They alight upon the
buildings and fences as well as upon the ground.
They are *walkers.*" In a few days he obtained

one, and sent me the skin. It proved to be what I had anticipated, namely, the American pipit, or titlark, a slender brown bird, about the size of the sparrow, which passes through the States in the fall and spring, to and from its breeding haunts in the far north. They generally appear by twos and threes, or in small loose flocks, searching for food on banks and plowed ground. As they fly up, they show two or three white quills in the tail, like the vesper sparrow. Flying over, they utter a single chirp or cry every few rods. They breed in the bleak, moss-covered rocks of Labrador. It is reported that their eggs have also been found in Vermont, and I feel quite certain that I saw this bird in the Adirondack Mountains in the month of August. The male launches into the air, and gives forth a brief but melodious song, after the manner of all larks. They are *walkers*. This is a characteristic of but few of our land-birds. By far the greater number are *hoppers*. Note the track of the common snowbird; the feet are not placed one in front of the other, as in the track of the crow or partridge, but side and side. The sparrows, thrushes, warblers, woodpeckers, buntings, etc., are all hoppers. On the other hand, all aquatic or semi-aquatic birds are walkers. The plovers and sandpipers and snipes run rapidly. Among the land-birds, the grouse, pigeons, quails, larks, and various blackbirds walk. The swallows walk, also, whenever they use their feet at all, but very awkwardly. The larks walk with ease and grace. Note the meadowlark strutting about all day in the meadows.

Besides being walkers, the larks, or birds allied to the larks, all sing upon the wing, usually poised or circling in the air, with a hovering, tremulous flight. The meadowlark occasionally does this in the early part of the season. At such times its long-drawn note or whistle becomes a rich, amorous warble.

The bobolink, also, has both characteristics, and, notwithstanding the difference of form and build, etc., is very suggestive of the English skylark, as it figures in the books, and is, no doubt, fully its equal as a songster.

Of our small wood-birds we have three varieties east of the Mississippi, closely related to each other, which I have already spoken of, and which walk, and sing, more or less, on the wing, namely, the two species of water-thrush or wagtails, and the oven-bird or wood-wagtail. The latter is the most common, and few observers of the birds can have failed to notice its easy, gliding walk. Its other lark trait, namely, singing in the air, seems not to have been observed by any naturalist. Yet it is a well-established characteristic, and may be verified by any person who will spend a half hour in the woods where this bird abounds on some June afternoon or evening. I hear it very frequently after sundown, when the ecstatic singer can hardly be distinguished against the sky. I know of a high, bald-top mountain where I have sat late in the afternoon and heard them as often as one every minute. Sometimes the bird would be far below me, sometimes near at hand; and very frequently the singer would be hovering a hundred feet above the summit. He would start from the trees on one side of the open space, reach his climax in the air, and plunge down on the other side. His descent after the song is finished is very rapid, and precisely like that of the titlark when it sweeps down from its course to alight on the ground.

I first verified this observation some years ago. I had long been familiar with the song, but had only strongly suspected the author of it, when, as I was walking in the woods one evening, just as the leaves were putting out, I saw one of these birds but a few rods from me. I was saying to myself, half audibly, "Come, now, show off, if it is you; I have come to the woods expressly to settle this point," when it began to ascend, by short hops and flights, through the branches, uttering a sharp, preliminary chirp. I followed it with my eye; saw it mount into the air and circle over the woods; and saw it sweep down again and dive through the trees, almost to the very perch from which it had started.

As the paramount question in the life of a bird is the question of food, perhaps the most serious troubles our feathered neighbors encounter are early in the spring, after the supply of fat with which Nature stores every corner and by-place of the system, thereby anticipating the scarcity of food, has been exhausted, and the sudden and severe changes in the weather which occur at this season make unusual demands upon their vitality. No doubt many of the earlier birds die from starvation and exposure at this season. Among a troop of Canada sparrows which I came upon one March day, all of them evidently much reduced, one was so feeble that I caught it in my hand.

During the present season, a very severe cold spell the first week in March drove the bluebirds to seek shelter about the houses and outbuildings. As night approached, and the winds and the cold increased, they seemed filled with apprehension and alarm, and in the outskirts of the city came about the windows and doors, crept behind the blinds, clung to the gutters and beneath the cornice, flitted from porch to porch, and from house to house, seeking in vain for some safe retreat from the cold. The street pump, which had a small opening just over the handle, was an attraction which they could not resist. And yet they seemed aware of the insecurity of the position; for no sooner would they stow themselves away into the interior of the pump, to the number of six or eight, than they would rush out again, as if apprehensive of some approaching danger. Time after time the cavity was filled and refilled, with blue and brown intermingled, and as often emptied. Presently they tarried longer than usual, when I made a sudden sally and captured three, that found a warmer and safer lodging for the night in the cellar.

In the fall, birds and fowls of all kinds become very fat. The squirrels and mice lay by a supply of food in their dens and retreats, but the birds, to a considerable extent, especially our winter residents, carry an equivalent in their own systems, in the form of adipose tissue. I killed a red-shouldered hawk one December, and on removing the skin found the body completely encased in a coating of fat one quarter of an inch in thickness. Not a particle of muscle was visible. This coating not only serves as a protection against the cold, but supplies the waste of the system when food is scarce or fails altogether.

The crows at this season are in the same condition. It is estimated that a crow needs at least half a pound of meat per day, but it is evident that for weeks and months during the winter and spring they must subsist on a mere fraction of that amount. I have no doubt that a crow or hawk, when in his fall condition, would live two weeks without a morsel of food passing his beak ; a domestic fowl will do as much. One January I unwittingly shut a hen under the door of an outbuilding, where not a particle of food could be obtained, and where she was entirely unprotected from the severe cold. When the luckless Dominick was discovered, about eighteen days afterward, she was brisk and lively, but fearfully pinched up, and as light as a bunch of feathers. The slightest wind carried her before it. But by judicious feeding she was soon restored.

The circumstance of the bluebirds being emboldened by the cold suggests the fact that the fear of man, which now seems like an instinct in the birds, is evidently an acquired trait, and foreign to them in a state of primitive nature. Every gunner has observed, to his chagrin, how wild the pigeons become after a few days of firing among them; and, to his delight, how easy it is to approach near his game in new or unfrequented woods. Professor Baird [1] tells me that a correspondent of theirs visited a small island in the Pacific Ocean, situated about two hundred miles off Cape St. Lucas, to procure specimens. The island was but a few miles in extent, and had probably never been visited half a dozen times by human beings. The naturalist found the birds and water-fowls so tame that it was but a waste of ammunition to shoot them. Fixing a noose on the end of a long stick, he captured them by putting it over their necks and hauling them to him. In some cases not even this contrivance was needed. A species of mockingbird in particular,

[1] Then at the head of the Smithsonian Institution.

larger than ours and a splendid songster, made itself so familiar as to be almost a nuisance, hopping on the table where the collector was writing, and scattering the pens and paper. Eighteen species were found, twelve of them peculiar to the island.

Thoreau relates that in the woods of Maine the Canada jay will sometimes make its meal with the lumbermen, taking the food out of their hands.

Yet, notwithstanding the birds have come to look upon man as their natural enemy, there can be little doubt that civilization is on the whole favorable to their increase and perpetuity, especially to the smaller species. With man come flies and moths, and insects of all kinds in greater abundance; new plants and weeds are introduced, and, with the clearing up of the country, are sowed broadcast over the land.

The larks and snow buntings that come to us from the north subsist almost entirely upon the seeds of grasses and plants; and how many of our more common and abundant species are field-birds, and entire strangers to deep forests?

In Europe some birds have become almost domesticated, like the house sparrow; and in our own country the cliff swallow seems to have entirely abandoned ledges and shelving rocks, as a place to nest, for the eaves and projections of farm and other outbuildings.

After one has made the acquaintance of most of

the land-birds, there remain the seashore and its
treasures. How little one knows of the aquatic
fowls, even after reading carefully the best authori-
ties, was recently forced home to my mind by the
following circumstance: I was spending a vacation
in the interior of New York, when one day a stranger alighted before the house, and with a cigar
box in his hand approached me as I sat in the
doorway. I was about to say that he would waste
his time in recommending his cigars to me, as I
never smoked, when he said that, hearing I knew
something about birds, he had brought me one
which had been picked up a few hours before in a
hay-field near the village, and which was a stranger
to all who had seen it. As he began to undo the
box I expected to see some of our own rarer birds,
perhaps the rose-breasted grosbeak or Bohemian
chatterer. Imagine, then, how I was taken aback
when I beheld instead a swallow-shaped bird, quite
as large as a pigeon, with forked tail, glossy black
above and snow-white beneath. Its parti-webbed
feet, and its long graceful wings, at a glance told
that it was a sea-bird; but as to its name or habitat
I must defer my answer till I could get a peep into
Audubon, or some large collection.

The bird had fallen down exhausted in a meadow,
and was picked up just as the life was leaving its
body. The place must have been one hundred and
fifty miles from the sea as the bird flies. As it

was the sooty tern, which inhabits the Florida Keys,
its appearance so far north and so far inland may
be considered somewhat remarkable. On removing
the skin I found it terribly emaciated. It had no
doubt starved to death, ruined by too much wing.
Another Icarus. Its great power of flight had made
it bold and venturesome, and had carried it so far
out of its range that it starved before it could return.

The sooty tern is sometimes called the sea-swal-
low on account of its form and power of flight. It
will fly nearly all day at sea, picking up food from
the surface of the water. There are several species
of terns, some of them strikingly beautiful.

1868.

INDEX

INDEX

INDEX

INDEX

INDEX

INDEX

INDEX

Printed in the United States
44036LVS00006B/60